VISUAL & PERFORMING ARTS

D0096001

Fringe Science

Fringe Science

PARALLEL UNIVERSES, WHITE TULIPS, AND MAD SCIENTISTS

EDITED BY

KEVIN R. GRAZIER

SMART
POP

An Imprint of BenBella Books, Inc.

Dallas, Texas

THIS PUBLICATION HAS NOT BEEN PREPARED, APPROVED, OR LICENSED BY ANY ENTITY THAT CREATED OR PRODUCED THE WELL-KNOWN TELEVISION SHOW *FRINGE*.

All rights reserved. No part of this book may be used or reproduced in any manner whatsoever without written permission except in the case of brief quotations embodied in critical articles or reviews.

Smart Pop is an Imprint of BenBella Books, Inc.
10300 N. Central Expressway, Suite 400
Dallas, TX 75231
www.benbellabooks.com
www.smartpopbooks.com
Send feedback to feedback@benbellabooks.com

Printed in the United States of America
10 9 8 7 6 5 4 3 2 1

Library of Congress Cataloging-in-Publication Data is available for this title.
ISBN 978-1-935618-68-3

Copyediting by Erica Lovett
Proofreading by Michael Fedison
Cover design by The Book Designers
Text design and composition by Neuwirth & Associates, Inc.
Printed by Bang

Distributed by Perseus Distribution
http://www.perseusdistribution.com/

To place orders through Perseus Distribution:
Tel: (800) 343-4499
Fax: (800) 351-5073
E-mail: orderentry@perseusbooks.com

Significant discounts for bulk sales are available. Please contact Glenn Yeffeth at glenn@benbellabooks.com or (214) 750-3628.

R05025 15200

COPYRIGHT ACKNOWLEDGMENTS

"Paranormal Is the New Normal" Copyright © 2011 by David Thomas

"In Search of *Fringe*'s Literary Ancestors" Copyright © 2011 by Amy H. Sturgis

"The Return of 1950s Science Fiction in *Fringe*" Copyright © 2011 by Paul Levinson

"Parallel Universes" Copyright © 2011 by Max Tegmark

"Déjà New" Copyright © 2011 by Mike Brotherton

"The Malleability of Memory" Copyright © 2011 by Garth Sundem

"*Fringe* Diseases" Copyright © 2011 by Jovana Grbić

"The Fringes of Neurotechnology" Copyright © 2011 by Brendan Allison

"Of White Tulips and Wormholes" Copyright © 2011 by Stephen Cass

"Moo" Copyright © 2011 by Amy Berner

"Waltered States" Copyright © 2011 by Nick Mamatas

"*Fringe* Double-Blinded Me with Science" Copyright © 2011 by Robert T. Jeschonek

"Massive Dynamic" Materials Copyright © 2011 by Jacob Clifton

Introduction Copyright © 2011 by Kevin R. Grazier
Other Materials Copyright © 2011 by BenBella Books, Inc.

CONTENTS

INTRODUCTION

Among the many scientific premises and science-fiction themes explored weekly in the television series *Fringe*, as well as within this anthology, one concept not explicitly addressed in an episode to date is that of chaos. At the same time one could easily make the argument that the entire series is a study in chaos theory, and no single episode makes explicit reference simply because its influence is interwoven throughout the fabric of the entire series.

A colloquial definition of the term *chaos* might include descriptors like disorder, disarray, and/or randomness: the disarray of Walter Bishop's laboratory or a Harvard fraternity house on Saturday morning being good examples. The definition advanced by a scientist or mathematician, on the other hand, would have less do to with disorder, nothing to do with randomness, and everything with predictability.

Dynamical systems—physical systems with many interacting parts—are all around us and a part of our everyday lives: billiard balls on a table, gas molecules in the room, a pendulum clock, our weather, the Solar System. A dynamical system is said to be chaotic when the solutions to the differential equations that govern its behavior are extremely sensitive to initial conditions: an ever-so-slight change, or perturbation, in the starting point leads to dramatically different outcomes or behaviors. A classic model for a chaotic system, and certainly the most familiar, is the weather, which exhibits behavior known as the Butterfly Effect. (After all, how many physical phenomena have movies named after them?) The notion is that weather is so sensitive to its initial state that a butterfly flapping its wings in Hong Kong one day can influence the weather in New York a week later. The more chaotic the system, the more pronounced are the effects of small perturbations like those from the efforts of a butterfly and the more difficult it is to predict the final outcome. The Universe is filled with small perturbations, and systems that behave in this manner are both commonplace and everywhere.

A dynamical system does not have to be as complex as Earth's weather to exhibit chaotic behavior, and some surprisingly simple systems are chaotic. A simple pendulum is not chaotic; a double pendulum—where a second free-swinging pendulum is attached to the mass of the first—is. On a pool table, hit the cue ball at two ever-so-slightly different angles, wind up with two different final arrangements that look entirely unrelated.

The notion of randomness doesn't even enter this chaotic landscape, at least not in an obvious way. Hit the cue ball the same way every single time, and you'll wind up with the exact same final state every single time. From a more pragmatic viewpoint, if you tried to repeat the experiment it's highly unlikely that every ball would begin the trial in exactly the same position on the table, or in the exact same orientation. It's equally unlikely that you'd hit the ball *exactly* the same way two successive times. In even a fairly simple chaotic system, these small differences matter.

The decisions we make on a daily basis can be viewed similarly, as perturbations to the paths of our lives—forks in the road known in chaos theory as bifurcations—with different, sometimes very different, possible outcomes. For example, how many times after a traumatic event has somebody involved lamented, "If only I hadn't..." "If only I'd have set my alarm clock somewhere away from my bedside when I thought about it, I wouldn't have slept through that final exam" (this example happened to me), or "If only I'd put a label on that coke bottle to indicate that it really contained antifreeze, you wouldn't have drank it" (this actually happened to two astronomer friends of mine). According to *Fringe* executive producer J.H. Wyman, "Your life is what your choices are."

Now here's where it gets weird. One cosmological model of parallel universes (discussed later in essays by both Max Tegmark and Mike Brotherton, and one taken seriously by theoretical physicists) posits that, whenever you are presented with a choice, "Do I do X or do I do Y?" parallel universes come into being in which every eventuality actually plays out. If we had a bird's-eye view of both universes, we could see that some choices are relatively inconsequential: the states of the two universes merge after a time and become identical. For most decisions, however, the two paths diverge—for some they diverge exponentially.

What is novel about *Fringe* is that the viewer sees two versions of "what might have been." We have that bird's-eye view, and are witness to the bifurcation and divergence of two lives, two Walter Bishops. Both Walter Bishops lost a son—one from disease, one at the hands of the other—and the path of their lives went in dramatically different and initially unpredictable ways. This is the hallmark of chaos, yet this is not a new concept in works of science fiction. For years works of television and cinematic science fiction have been presenting viewers with an implicit worldview in which the flow of time is chaotic by its very nature. How often have time travelers observed, or counseled fellow travelers, that caution is in order because changing the past, even through something as trivial as stepping on an ant, could result in a dramatically different future?

The divergence of the lives of Walter Bishop, initiated by the events surrounding the illness of his son(s), Peter, have left us with a harder, edgier, more militaristic Walternate in the other universe, and a Walter in this Universe who, quite literally, has a hole in his head and uses LSD as his experimental drug of choice. This is an intentional element on the series: in an October 2010 interview in the *New York Post*, *Fringe* executive producer Jeff Pinkner said that the creators of the series built a parallel universe to show "how small choices that you make define you as a person and can change your life in large ways down the line." (On this point Nick Mamatas observes in detail in his essay "Waltered States" how the two different versions of Walter Bishop mimic the personalities of 1960s icons and rivals G. Gordon Liddy and Timothy Leary.) Events gave rise to two very different Walters, yet clearly the seeds of both of these disparate personalities must have been present in both, at least in small measure, to start.

As we bounce from human interaction to human interaction in life, like billiard balls on a table, who we are, the choices we make, and the repercussions of our actions can create pronounced and unpredictable ripple effects in the lives of those around us. Those effects—perturbations to the lives of others, if you will— can create secondary ripples, tertiary ripples, and so forth, having unintended and unpredictable consequences even in the lives of people we've never even met. So although it's not surprising that aspects of Walternate's personality might be mirrored in the persona of others in his close sphere of influence—like Fauxlivia (she of the Olympic marksmanship medal)—somebody in the right place at the right time might, intentionally or otherwise, have profound influence over lives and events that are far more wide-ranging. A traffic accident on a Los Angeles freeway at the wrong time of day can literally disrupt hundreds of thousands of lives dramatically and almost instantaneously. How many missed dinners, missed dentist appointments, missed airline boardings, missed soccer practices, missed therapy sessions, missed recitals, or missed dates arise from a single ill-advised lane change?

Walter Bishop's and William Bell's human trials with cortexiphan, and other radical scientific experimentation, certainly had far-flung impacts: outcomes (i.e. "The Pattern") that drove much of the action on *Fringe*, particularly in the first season. This ripple effect is arguably even more pronounced Over There: take an otherwordly brilliant scientist, subject him to a traumatic event like the loss/theft of his son, and he might just convince himself to be the change he wants to see in his world. In that sense, the entirety of Walternate's life can be viewed as a perturbation to the evolution of his entire society.[1] Compared to society in this Universe, the Unites States Over There has grown colder, harsher, more militaristic, an evolution with marked similarity to Walternate's own.

---

1 Strictly speaking, the divergence of two societies, filled with individuals capable of making choices, is, more correctly, what's known as a *complex system* rather than a chaotic system. The definition of complexity is, however, itself so complex—and not universally agreed upon—that we'll stick to the much simpler notion of chaos here.

An object or system that is self-similar in this way—one that has a similar appearance at different size scales—is said to be fractal. Mountains are fractal. So are snowflakes. This is another hallmark of a chaotic system and another manner in which *Fringe* can be viewed as a study in chaos theory. That the lives of the characters on *Fringe* can be considered a real-world gedanken experiment on the chaotic nature of the choices we make, when those characters themselves experiment upon others, is another way in which *Fringe* can be said to be fractal. The *Fringe* writers experiment with the lives of the Walter Bishops in the same way that Walter Bishop experimented on his cortexiphan victim subjects. (In his essay "*Fringe* Double-Blinded Me with Science" Robert T. Jeschonek explores in much greater detail fictional and real-world aspects of experimentation within *Fringe*.)

We see within the self-similar structure of a snowflake that order can arise from within chaotic systems. In some there are even "preferred" states, states to which the system tends to gravitate irrespective of starting point. These are called attractors. Though the two *Fringe* universes have undergone marked divergence, they're not *entirely* different. There are some events that simply have so much weight, so much gravity, that they cannot be changed. They will happen even in societies that have shown pronounced divergence.[2] The attacks of 9/11 were such events, *Fringe* suggests; the destruction of the World Trade Center was not (Over There, the Pentagon and White House alone were attacked). Even from "The Pattern," which initially didn't seem like it had a pattern at all, we see order arising from chaos on

---

2 Fans of the series *Doctor Who* will note that this concept has been broached several times since the series' continuation—in that series attractors are called "fixed points."

Fringe. In that way, even the real-world television series is self-similar to the events depicted within the *Fringe* universe.

Order from disorder, self-similarity, extreme divergence of nearly similar states: the chaotic elements of *Fringe* are implicit within its framework. The show is certainly far more than a gedanken experiment in chaos theory, however, and the essays that follow easily make that case. In the pages to come Paul Levinson, Amy H. Sturgis, and David Dylan Thomas discuss the rich mythos of *Fringe*, one informed by countless seminal works—pillars from science fiction past. For the hard-core technology fans of *Fringe*, you'll find plenty of meaty essays into which you can sink your teeth—and although I do not refer to Gene here, Amy Berner does provide a very charming essay on Walter's bovine companion. The fringe science and technology explored weekly on *Fringe* is, itself, explored here in essays by Stephen Cass (time travel), Jovana Grbić (infectious diseases), Brendan Allison (brain-computer interfaces), and Garth Sundem (memory manipulation). I hope that you, as much as I, enjoy exploring the technology, the really "out there" (or Over There) concepts, and even the chaos that, like a chemical reaction in Walter's laboratory, combine to give us *Fringe* science.

KEVIN R. GRAZIER
Los Angeles, CA
May 2011

PARANORMAL IS THE
NEW NORMAL

DAVID DYLAN THOMAS

In television and cinema science fiction we're frequently exposed to paranormal phenomena, the source of which the viewer eventually learns is mysticism, the supernatural, or the Occult. Such works, then, belong more in the overarching realm of speculative fiction rather than *science* fiction. On *Fringe* we are constantly fed a similar diet of phenomena, like precognition, telekinesis, clairvoyance, and astral projection, but always given a physical basis that defers to the scientific and rational. Based upon this, David Dylan Thomas argues that *Fringe* rightfully earns its place firmly within the realm of *science* fiction.

The *Fringe* Files

On September 9, 2008, *Fringe* premiered on Fox, the same network that launched *The X-Files* fifteen years earlier (almost to the day). The two shows seemed to share a lot in common: in both, a specialty division of the FBI investigates paranormal activity, applying scientific rigor and professional investigation techniques to the bizarre and unexplained. There is even a no-nonsense female lead new to all these strange goings-on about to be taken on a journey that will change her life. It seemed *Fringe* would have little to distinguish itself from its groundbreaking kith, until a pattern—if you'll excuse the phrase—began to emerge.

Within its first season, *The X-Files'* investigators had encountered ghosts, mediums, reincarnation, faith healing, werewolves, and, well, whatever you call it when a twin is psychically controlled by his dead brother's frozen head ("Roland," 1-23). Within its first season, *Fringe* covered exactly two of these topics: ghosts ("The Equation," 1-8) and mediums ("The Ghost Network," 1-3)—and in neither case were they faced with the real deal. *The X-Files* would go on to tackle vampires, the Devil, zombies, and God. In its entire run so far, *Fringe* has tackled exactly none of these.

Two Flavors of Weird

When paranormal stuff happens in fiction—or real life, for that matter—we tend to blame one of two culprits: the supernatural or the scientific. If we see a magician pull a rabbit out of a hat, either he has mystical powers that science cannot explain or he's simply opened a portal to another universe that is, for some reason, overrun with rabbits. *Fringe* would prefer to believe the latter. It is not interested in the paranormal as it pertains to the supernatural. In fact, if you look at the title sequence, the show makes itself quite clear on exactly what it believes constitutes paranormal activity. The list of words that go floating by include, in season one:

> Psychokinesis
> Teleportation
> Nanotechnology
> Artificial Intelligence
> Precognition
> Dark Matter
> Suspended Animation
> Cybernetics
> Transmogrification

And in season two:

> Hypnosis
> ESP
> Hive Mind

Pyrokinesis
Neuroscience
Clairaudience
Cryonics
Parallel Universes
Astral Projection
Mutation
Protoscience
Genetic Engineering

Nowhere do we see vampirism, lycanthropy, the undead, or spectrology (the study of ghosts).

The title itself expresses the limit of the show's paranormal jurisdiction. *Fringe* refers to the term "fringe science." The phenomena the team explores are on the fringe of science, but are still, by definition, within the boundaries of science.

A Ghost by Any Other Name

The focus of the series can be best expressed by the episodes in which Fringe Division ostensibly concerns itself with supernatural phenomena, only to explain it away using science. In "The Ghost Network," the team encountered Roy McComb, a man who believed his ability to predict horrible events came from communication with the Devil. What was actually happening was that Roy, experimented on earlier by Walter Bishop, had a compound in his blood that allowed him to receive transmissions on a secret radio frequency used by normal human beings who were planning these events. The "medium" was simply a living antenna. In "The Equation," a boy believed he was seeing his dead mother come back to life but was in fact strapped to a machine that created hallucinations. In *Fringe*, ghosts are just electrical impulses in the brain.

Even your garden-variety monsters take on some weird scientific ontology in the *Fringe*-iverse. The closest the team has ever gotten to a vampire was a spinal fluid–sucking victim of experimentation ("Midnight," 1-18). The closest it has ever gotten to a werewolf was a designer virus that turned a man into a beast ("The Transformation," 1-13). Shape-shifting, common in many folklores (including vampire and werewolf myths), manifests itself in the series as cybernetic soldiers from an alternate universe who take on the forms of friends and loved ones to infiltrate our world. Even though they are explicitly referred to by the more mythical-sounding moniker "shape-shifters," their technological roots are quite literally skin deep, as demonstrated whenever an injury reveals the mercury that courses through their veins.

The Post-Paranormal World

So why not do an episode about zombies that are actually zombies or ghosts that are actually ghosts? It worked for *The X-Files*. Why would a show limit itself to the narrative possibilities offered by science fiction and not include the potential plot twists available in supernatural horror? Part of the reason may stem from the difference between telling spooky stories in 2008 versus telling spooky stories in 1993.

In 1993, a vampire was a vampire was a vampire. In the popular culture, Francis Ford Coppola's gothic take on *Dracula* had hit theaters the year before and Neil Jordan's film adaptation of *Interview with a Vampire* was still a year away. We were just beginning to wrap our minds around treating a vampire as a sympathetic character, or at least as an antihero, but at the end of the day, a vampire was a scary (albeit sexy) dude who sucked your blood.

In 2008, a vampire is, if not everyman, then at least eminently relatable for a number of reasons. First off, they're all over television, novels, and movies—*True Blood*, *Twilight*, and *The Vampire Diaries*, and in years prior, *Buffy the Vampire Slayer*, *Angel*, and *Blade*. Secondly, they're all warm and cuddly. Each of those titles I just mentioned contains sympathetic vampire protagonists. Not antiheroes. Just plain old heroes. Thirdly, and most importantly, vampires are unliving out loud. In the world of *True Blood*, vampires are a part of everyday life. If a character runs into one, they don't have to worry about someone else not believing the encounter took place. Vampires are just . . . normal.

Pop culture's attitude adjustment toward the undead doesn't stop there. Zombies are the new vampires. They're the stars of the critically acclaimed, ratings record-breaking television series *The Walking Dead*, itself an adaptation of a wildly popular comic book. The 2004 film *Dawn of the Dead* found both box office and critical success. It was considered to be one of the few horror remakes worth watching, and launched the career of director Zack Snyder (*300*, *Watchmen*) to boot. They've even been woven into the literary fabric with the best seller *Pride and Prejudice and Zombies*, which itself has launched a subgenre of horror/classic mash-ups including *Sense and Sensibility and Sea Monsters* and, of course, *Abraham Lincoln: Vampire Hunter*, which, like *Prejudice*, will be made into a feature film. And zombies can do more than scare us now. They can make us laugh. *Zombieland, Shaun of the Dead, Fido, Dead and Breakfast*, and *Dead Snow* all represent entries in the new "Zom Com" or "Zombedy" subgenre.

There seems little sport—and even less fear—in doing an episode about zombies or vampires when they all pretty much have their own agents now.

Fringe Knows What Scares You

The other difference between telling scary stories in the early '90s versus the late '00s is what scares us. In the early '90s our obsession with technology was, relatively speaking, nascent. The internet was only just taking root (*The X-Files* was, in fact, one of the first television shows to benefit from online fandom), and our gadget-mongering was still limited to the relatively new innovation known as the mobile phone (a staple Mulder and Scully accessory). Today, the myriad ways in which we interact with technology both fascinate and unsettle us. In the last ten years, the human genome has been mapped, computers have been placed in virtually every object (including our own bodies), wireless communication has infiltrated nearly every corner of the map, and the rate of data accumulation has accelerated to five exabytes every two days (that's as much data as was collected between the dawn of man and 2003). Each of these advances gives us as much cause for trepidation as celebration, resulting in a sort of mystical reverence for technology: a veneration that combines both senses of the term—respect and terror—and which supplants the mysticism of the truly

mystical. Put simply, the supernatural is no longer as frightening as the technological.

The X-Files had its share of technophobia—computers gone
mad ("Ghost in the Machine," 1-7), genetic tampering ("Young
at Heart," 1-16), engineered superviruses ("F. Emasculate," 2-22),
bioengineering ("War of the Coprophages," 3-12)—but these
were only a part of the mix. *Fringe* devotes itself exclusively to
the ways in which technology can kill us. In particular, it dwells
on the question of what happens when we experiment on
ourselves. In many cases, the root cause of the phenomenon
being investigated is an experiment Walter had a hand in himself.
It is as if, when offered the classic universal monster tableau that
includes Dracula, the Mummy, and the Wolf Man, the writers
chose to focus exclusively on Frankenstein.

As if to drive this point home, one of the ongoing mysteries of
season one was the meaning of the letters ZFT, which were
revealed in "Ability" (1-14) to stand for the title of a book,
Zerstörung durch Fortschritte der Technologie. This translates
roughly to "destruction by advancement of technology." The title
amounts to a *Fringe* narrative mission statement. And, as the
show demonstrates, there are many different ways in which that
destruction can unfold.

Your Own Worst Enemy

A decade into the twenty-first century, we know more about the
human body than ever before. But with that knowledge comes
the ability to cause more damage than ever before. This tension
makes body horror—a horror subgenre in which terror derives

from the degeneration or mutilation of the body, often via disease or experimentation—a particularly potent vessel for *Fringe* plotlines. From the flesh-dissolving contagion of the pilot to the grotesque body-mods of the time traveling Alistair Peck in "White Tulip" (2-18), what can happen to our bodies—or what we can do to our own—is a pervasive fear.

A particularly striking example appears in "Ability," in which a toxin was synthesized to cause all of a victim's orifices to seal shut, thus suffocating them. This resonates in two ways: One, the toxin worked by causing the body's scar tissue mechanism to go into overdrive, sealing any gap in skin tissue, thus using something that is meant to heal us to kill us. Our own body used against us. Two, it left its victims effectively faceless, echoing our own fears about being rendered without identity by technology. In both ways, we were betrayed by the very technology meant to save us.

Even major characters have technology-related health issues. Recurring season-one villain Mr. Jones found himself dying slowly after using a teleportation device invented by Walter. Nina Sharp lost an arm to Walter's universe-crossing machine. Walter's own mental issues were traced back to having parts of his brain removed and added to other people via advanced technology.

In the Army Now

One of the scariest stories we can read in the newspaper is that a terrorist organization or enemy country is closer than we are to developing some sort of technology that can cause us harm.

Even when our own country develops formidable military tech, we can't help but wonder how long it will be before that same tech is used against us.

These anxieties manifest in interesting and sometimes paradoxical ways on the show. Not only does the idea of shape-shifting take on a strictly scientific form, as stated before, but it takes on a peculiarly militaristic one as well. Here, the imagined tech reflects a military fear that is, ironically, not the result of technology in the real world. The threat posed by the shape-shifters is that you'll never know who one is until it is too late. This taps into the very basic military fear of not knowing who the enemy is (a pervasive J.J. Abrams trope). In the War on Terror, the fear abroad is not being able to distinguish civilians from combatants, while at home the paranoia centers on being unable to distinguish sleepers from citizens.

The most potent examples of this dilemma defined the initial arc of seasons two and three. Season two opened with Agent Charlie Francis being replaced by a shape-shifting soldier from the alternate universe, deceiving everyone, including Olivia Dunham, who was closer to him than any of the other regulars. Season three opened with an even more intimate and prolonged deception, when Olivia from the alternate universe replaced our own, deceiving her lover, Peter Bishop, who had grown closer to the real Olivia than anyone. *Fringe* takes the paranoia of not knowing if the stranger in the airport is a terrorist and extends it to the person sharing your bed.

Of course, technology need not be new to be scary. Suicide bombers have been around since at least the 1880s, but their prevalence in modern warfare has put them front and center in the public amygdala. It is no wonder, then, that the concept of a weaponized human has appeared in several episodes: "Fracture" (2-3); "The Cure" (1-6); and "The Road Not Taken" (1-19). "Fracture" was the most explicit of these metaphors. The victims, injected with a serum that turned them into living explosives that shattered when a particular radio frequency was transmitted, were in fact being used to send a message by a rogue military commander. Olivia and Peter even traveled to Iraq to find the root of the serum, which originated as an attempt to counter chemicals used by Saddam himself.

That technology can turn us into weapons, even without our knowledge, is an all-too-real scenario that *Fringe* exploits. Peter himself is the greatest human weapon the show has produced to date. The doomsday devices that dominate season three are inextricably linked to him, unable to function without at least some of his DNA. When he was fully integrated with one of the machines in the season-three finale, "The Day We Died," it destroyed an entire universe. The design of the devices suggests that in modern warfare, it is the complete integration of man and machine that holds the greatest destructive—and redemptive, given Peter's ability to use the machine to bridge the universes—potential.

What's in the Box?

Then there is, of course, what we usually think of when we think of technology: iPads, cell phones, laptops, camcorders. You know, gadgets. Or, in the world of *Fringe*, killer gadgets. The mysterious cylinders of "The Arrival" (1-4); the window that Walter ultimately used to cross over into a parallel universe in

"Peter" (2-16); the doomsday devices both sides built throughout season three. This flavor of technophobia is as old as the atomic bomb, but its pervasiveness in the show suggests that there is no scientific leap forward that cannot cause untold, if not unforeseen, damage.

Perhaps the most deliberately metaphorical instance of this fear was represented by "The Box" (3-2), in which a mysterious container killed those who opened it (and anyone nearby). On any other show, we'd be dealing with something mystical, like Pandora's Box or the Ark of the Covenant, but this box did its damage using an ultrasonic wave. Given the mystical reverence we have for technology, though, the "how" is almost beside the point. Most consumer technology today comes in the form of a closed box. An iPod, a laptop, a DVR. We don't know what's inside, and we don't particularly care, as long as it does what we want it to. But the mystery inside the box has never been greater. Even if you can't guess what all the parts of a car do, they're at least differentiated. Break open an iPod and you simply see more "boxes." That the eponymous box caused harm using invisible waves simply enhanced the mystical aura and echoed the very real fears people have about modern technology causing internal, invisible harm. A thresher can rip your arm off, but a cell phone can give you brain cancer.

Yes, We Have No Aliens

The most pervasive villains on *The X-Files* that have made no appearance on *Fringe* are, of course, aliens. In many cases, when some paranormal activity victimized some poor, unsuspecting citizen of the *X-Files* universe, the most likely explanation was that aliens (or aliens in league with the government) did it. On *Fringe*, this is never the case. The most likely explanation on that show is someone from a parallel universe did it.

Both explanations offer an easy way to explain the use of technology vastly superior to our own. Aliens are, technologically speaking, very much like alternate universe humans. They have different technology because they evolved differently. But where aliens speak to a fear of the external and foreign, alternate universe humans speak to a fear of the familiar and, ultimately, of the self. Instead of xenophobia, you get autophobia.

"Jacksonville" (2-15) demonstrated what people who look, talk, and act just like us are really capable of. Scientists from an alternate universe caused two identical buildings from different universes to merge, inflicting horrible deaths on those within. It is, in fact, because the buildings (and the people within) are so similar that the experiment took place at all (an attempt to exchange equal mass between universes). In that sense it was similarity itself that killed, but this episode took that idea one step further. Not only were characters similar to our heroes to be feared, but so were our heroes themselves.

In an attempt to fight back and discover when the next incident like this would occur, Walter took Olivia back to Jacksonville, Florida, where she had been given experimental drugs as a child to enhance her innate abilities. These clandestine experiments involved scores of children, many of whom were haunted for the rest of their lives (and some of whom became the "monsters" of previous episodes). While it is horrible to imagine that some alien race could come down from the heavens and abduct our children and run experiments on them, it is perhaps more frightening to imagine that human beings, *fighting for our side*, could do the same. And while *The X-Files* often depicted human complicity in such atrocities, *Fringe* lays the blame exclusively on people, whichever world they come from.

This is the fear, and the lesson, that *Fringe* taps into. Dr. Frankenstein was not an alien or a supernatural creature. He was a person.

That alone, of course, is not what made him dangerous. *Fringe* might suggest that there are two more factors at play—two more things you need to understand about Dr. Frankenstein that made him a threat. The first is that he was very, very smart.

Smarter Than Your Average Theoretical Physicist

In "White Tulip," brilliant scientist Alistair Peck discovered how to travel through time at the cost of dozens of human lives. Geneticist and former cell decay and regeneration specialist Roland David Barrett actually brought someone back from the dead, but only after some vicious—albeit impressive—organ thievery in "Marionette" (3-9). If either of these or any number of other *Fringe* antagonists were only of even average intelligence they would have done far less damage. But intelligence is not the only ingredient necessary for paranormal chaos.

This is because even a smart person poses no threat when their intentions are pure, or even mundane. We have GPS, in part, because researchers at MIT got bored one day and tried to track the position of Sputnik for a lark. The real danger, *Fringe* seems to say, is when you combine human endeavor at its finest with human frailty at its basest. What Peck, Barrett, and Frankenstein all have in common—in addition to genius—is grief. And the show's loudest warning about mixing profound emotional wounds with profound intellectual curiosity is Walter Bishop himself.

The Fault Lies
Not in the Technology . . .

If *Fringe* has a lynchpin episode, it is "Peter." In this episode we saw the root of the show's overall narrative. Walter Bishop, grieving father to a son claimed by disease, opened a portal to another world. There he saw his opposite number about to face the same tragedy. Only this time a cure was found—and destroyed—all while the alternate universe Walter (cleverly dubbed "Walternate") was looking the other way. In order to save Walternate's son, Walter broke through to the other universe and stole him. On this side, he cured him, but never gave him back. He couldn't bear to lose his son again, even if it wasn't really his son.

All of the threats posed by the alternate universe to our own—and vice versa—began with this one simple act of grief.

Technology amplifies the consequence of emotion. This sentiment is, perhaps, the greatest fear and the greatest hope proposed by *Fringe*. In this sense the show becomes a plea for responsible science, for science itself does not bring about the horrors our heroes investigate on the show (in fact it routinely provides the solution). It merely enables the greed and fear of ordinary humans to exact far more catastrophic consequences than they might otherwise be capable of. In the end, it's not the insatiable hunger of vampires and zombies we need to worry about, nor is it the fearsome reach of technology and medicine; it's the simple human frailty of our best and brightest.

DAVID DYLAN THOMAS has a confession to make. He didn't actually like *Fringe* when he first saw it. He felt the same way about *The X-Files*, though, and has now seen every episode of each. When he's not giving shows a second chance, he directs films, manages websites, and cohosts podcasts in Pennsylvania. He tweets @movie_pundit and blogs at www.daviddylanthomas.com and www.straight-2dvdmovies.com, both of which he founded.

IN SEARCH OF *FRINGE*'S LITERARY ANCESTORS

AMY H. STURGIS

Sir Isaac Newton remarked, "If I have seen further it is only by standing on the shoulders of giants." Like a scientific journal article that builds upon previous works, the series *Fringe* borrows from, and pays clear homage to, many of the "giant" works of science fiction that preceded it. Sci-fi historian Amy H. Sturgis, PhD, examines the science-fiction influences that lay the foundation of *Fringe*.

On the night of September 9, 2008, I joined millions of other viewers in watching the premiere episode of *Fringe*. My first thought then remains my conviction now: *Fringe* is a show with unusually deep science-fiction roots. As a scholar as well as a fan of the genre, I find continual delight in watching *Fringe*. It's certainly a compelling series in its own right, but as many fans have discovered, it also can serve as a kind of "cultural literacy test" about the classic works that inform it.

The characters and dual universes in *Fringe* boast their own rich backstories, of course, but the show as a whole has a backstory, too: it builds on a centuries-deep foundation of science-fiction writings, most notably the literary traditions of the irresponsible scientist and the paranormal investigator. Some aspects of the series offer loud and loving tributes to the texts that obviously inspired them, while other allusions remain more subtle, tucked quietly between the lines of individual episodes. The identity of a few of the genre giants on whose shoulders *Fringe* stands might even surprise the show's producers and writers.

One thing is certain: Dr. Walter Bishop, Peter Bishop, FBI Agent Olivia Dunham, and FBI Junior Agent Astrid Farnsworth are characters with impressive literary (and, for that matter, television) ancestries. *Fringe* may be a cutting-edge series in many ways, but its grounding in the science-fiction tradition marks it as the most recent voice in a long and ongoing dialogue about what is possible, what is moral, and what is human.

Fringe: The New *Frankenstein*

Series cocreator J.J. Abrams is well aware of the debt *Fringe* owes to literature; in fact, he explicitly links the origin of the series to the very birth of modern science fiction itself. Most scholars today agree that the publication of Mary Wollstonecraft Shelley's 1818 masterpiece, *Frankenstein, or The Modern Prometheus*, marks the transition point at which so-called "proto-science fiction" ended and the full-fledged genre of contemporary science fiction began. The questions and concerns raised by that novel—including what responsibilities a creator should assume after the act of creation and what ethical limits if any should restrict the progress of scientific research—still lie at the heart of the genre today.

Fringe: *The Complete First Season* DVD set includes a featurette entitled "Evolution: The Genesis of *Fringe*." In this segment, Abrams explains that the original vision for the series entailed revisiting "the *Frankenstein* idea, but told as legitimately as possible." Telling the story "legitimately" included updating a central character by turning the aristocratic Genevan medical student Victor Frankenstein into the eccentric U.S. scientist Dr. Walter Bishop. Like Victor, Walter shuns the scientific consensus of the day, following his own genius into unorthodox, even illegal experimentation.

It's easy to see parallels between the two characters. Both brilliant scientists mean well: they desire to explore the very nature of reality itself and thus expand the boundaries of human knowledge. In Shelley's novel, Victor conducts research in order to discover the spark of life and re-create it. He dreams of humanity freed from mortality. Walter's experiments over his far longer career vary widely, but the main story arc of *Fringe* revolves around his choice to conduct research in order to save his son's life—or, more accurately, cheat his son's death. He dreams of Peter being healthy and safe.

To reach their desired goals, both use unethical methods. Victor plunders fresh graves to find human body parts for his laboratory and refuses to provide even the most basic of necessities to the life he creates. Walter escalates experiments with nootropic drugs on innocent children, leaving them with after-effects that continue into adulthood, and wholly ignores warnings that acting on his untested theories could, as his assistant Carla Warren tells him, "rupture the fundamental constants of nature" ("Peter," 2-16). Furthermore, each genius single-handedly makes decisions that determine the fate of many. Victor's neglected creation slays his friends and family members. Walter's recklessness costs the life of his assistant, drives his wife to suicide, and plunges an alternate world into chaos.

Perhaps most importantly, both Victor and Walter are haunted by their past scientific endeavors, pursued by the evidence of their own mistakes. Everywhere Victor looks, he finds the creature. Everywhere Walter looks, he finds evidence of an upcoming violent collision between our Universe and the other one Over There, a cataclysm that he set in motion when he opened the door between worlds and took the alternate Peter as his own son. Neither Victor nor Walter can escape the consequences of science pursued with intellectual arrogance, personal selfishness, and moral unaccountability. It's all too appropriate that Peter asks Olivia in that first episode: "You're telling me what? My father was Dr. Frankenstein?"

The difference between the characters of Victor and Walter—and perhaps this also is what Abrams means by reimagining the *Frankenstein* story "as legitimately as possible"—is one of redemption. In Shelley's story, Victor dies, leaving his cautionary tale as his only positive legacy. Walter, however, has the chance to try to contain some of the damage he's caused. He's released from the mental asylum where he's spent the last seventeen years in order to lend his unique expertise to the science team of the Fringe Division.

Through his investigations as part of this team, Walter not only learns the true scope of his experiments' results, but he also works to protect his world from further harm and stop the cycle of unintended consequences that his research has unleashed. Science may get us into serious trouble, the creators of the series seem to be saying, but science may also provide the much-needed answers to our most pressing questions. Perhaps the same mad scientist who first appeared to be a villain might look a bit more like a hero if given a second chance.

It's fitting that *Fringe*, like the genre of contemporary science fiction itself, traces its genesis back to *Frankenstein*. The ill-fated Victor is not, however, the only literary forerunner of the intrepid Fringe Division science team.

Ancestors: Early Science-Fiction Investigators

Today we find science-fiction and mystery novels in separate sections of the bookstore, and we don't think a thing about it. That wasn't always the case. Both the modern detective story and modern science fiction sprang from a common idea born of the Enlightenment: that the Universe could be understood through reason, and that using the proper investigative method would uncover the answer—whether the question was how to reach outer space or who killed the victim. In part, these genres also sprang from a common father, and for decades a number of writers blurred the lines between them, allowing the genres to inform and cross-fertilize each other during their formative years. This blending of the two genres is a tradition the creators of *Fringe* proudly continue.

Edgar Allan Poe, Ratiocination, and Genre

Modern science fiction may have one mother, Mary Wollstonecraft Shelley, but many men could lay claim to its paternity. One is Edgar Allan Poe, though he is perhaps better known for his works of Gothic horror. Jules Verne, himself an early and important figure in science fiction, praised Poe as the creator of the novel of scientific marvels. Verne even wrote a sequel novel (*An Antarctic Mystery, or The Sphinx of the Ice Fields*, 1897) to Poe's *The Narrative of Arthur Gordon Pym* (1838). Many of Poe's works are recognizable as what we today would call science fiction: for instance, "Eureka: A Prose Poem" (1848) anticipates scientific discoveries of the twentieth century as it seeks to explain the Universe, and "Mellonta Tauta" (1850) satirizes Poe's contemporary world from the vantage point of the year 2848.

A quick glance at the table of contents of Harold Beaver's edited collection *The Science Fiction of Edgar Allan Poe* (1976) reveals that Poe's science-fiction writings deal with mesmerism, galvanism, resurrection, and even time travel, among other ideas—all subjects, I should point out, that could easily be termed fringe science.

Besides being a pioneer of science fiction, Poe also was the father of the first detective in modern mystery fiction, C. Auguste Dupin. The French Dupin solved the cases of "The Murders in the Rue Morgue" (1841), "The Mystery of Marie Rogêt" (1842-1843), and "The Purloined Letter" (1844). Like Walter and Peter in *Fringe*, Dupin does not have, or want, a career in law enforcement. Instead, he consults on unusual cases that leave regular officials baffled. He's not a trained scientist, but his method of investigation is scientific in its precision. As he explains in "The Mystery of Marie Rogêt," it comprises "the most rigidly exact in science applied to the shadow and spirituality of the most intangible in speculation"—in other words, what Poe calls *ratiocination*, the marriage of rigorous reason and creative imagination. This is the key link between both Poe's works themselves and the genres they helped to inspire: the celebration of ratiocination is also a distinct hallmark of Poe's science fiction.

Applying logic and creativity to mysteries in the belief that the unknown can be known is a process any detective or scientist, fictional or real, would appreciate and recognize. It certainly sounds like what Walter does in his basement laboratory at Harvard University. In Poe's detective stories, it leads Dupin to put himself inside the criminal's mind in a process much like forensic psychologists use in criminal profiling today. With her likely forensic science training as a U.S. Marine Corps special investigator and an FBI agent, Olivia probably would feel right at home working on a case with Dupin.

At the heart of the investigative enterprise—whether scientific research or crime detection—is the Enlightenment's faith in an orderly universe. It follows that if we ask the right questions in the right ways, we can find the truth. Building on this premise, a number of other authors after Poe also chose to blur the lines between what we now consider to be the distinct genres of detective and science fiction. In so doing, these writers created characters who believed that it was possible to know the unknown and who used a combination of imagination and reason to this end. I'll call them science-fiction investigators. Together they paved the shadowy and mysterious ground that our heroes in *Fringe* now walk.

Literary Science-Fiction Investigators

In *Fringe*, Olivia, Walter, Peter, and Astrid devote their time to investigating bizarre events that cannot be explained through the traditional work of major law enforcement agencies. While many of these events seem to be related to Walter's previous research about and experience with the alternate universe, a number of others imply a coordinated scientific interest in our own Universe by an unknown and powerful third party. As Special Agent-in-Charge Phillip Broyles says, it's "as if someone out there is experimenting, only the whole world is their lab" ("Pilot," 1-1). Members of the Fringe Division, among others, call these mysterious happenings The Pattern. As of the conclusion of the third season, the exact relationship between The Pattern and Walter's earlier work remains to be seen.

All of these uncanny events, however, share something in common: to be understood, they must be examined by individuals who aren't constrained by mainstream assumptions about what is possible or impossible. In other words, if anyone is going to understand what's happening, it will be people who employ Poe's ratiocination: people who think methodically, rationally, and yet imaginatively, people outside of the proverbial box, people quite literally on the fringe of their disciplines. For the science team, this requires embracing fringe science, which, as Olivia explains to Peter, may include such bizarre subjects as "mind control, teleportation, astral projection, invisibility, genetic mutation, reanimation"—or, to use Peter's term, "pseudoscience" ("Pilot").

Walter's expertise in the subject of fringe science and the others' acceptance of its extreme possibilities marks these characters as the latest in an impressive line we can trace back to characters such as Poe's C. Auguste Dupin. But Dupin is not the only character of note; if anything, he started a popular trend. Doctor Giacomo Rappaccini appeared three years after Dupin in Nathaniel Hawthorne's short story "Rappaccini's Daughter" (*United States Magazine and Democratic Review*, 1844). To be fair, Rappaccini is less of a detective than a researcher in fringe science, but he certainly serves as a memorable precursor to Walter in *Fringe*. A brilliant scientist, Rappaccini conducts dangerous and controversial experiments that force him to live in isolation. Ultimately he jeopardizes his only child, Beatrice, whose life has become tainted by and inextricably bound up with his research.

When I reread the tragic tale now, I'm instantly reminded of the warnings inherent in the way *Fringe* portrays the intergenerational effects of Walter's irresponsible experimentation. His interference in the alternate world radically changes Peter's destiny, and his use of young Olivia in his tests with the drug cortexiphan alters her irrevocably. We can only hope that *Fringe* ends on a happier note than Hawthorne's story does.

Bram Stoker's classic novel *Dracula* (1897) introduced several memorable characters to popular culture. One of these is Professor Abraham Van Helsing, who is described (by Dr. John Seward to Arthur Holmwood) like this: "He is a seemingly arbitrary man, this is because he knows what he is talking about better than any one else. He is a philosopher and a metaphysician, and one of the most advanced scientists of his day, and he has, I believe, an absolutely open mind." If you add a predilection for strawberry milkshakes and hallucinogenic drugs, this description would also fit Walter. Van Helsing's broad-mindedness, as much as his medical and scientific knowledge, makes him invaluable in solving paranormal mysteries.

The last years of the nineteenth century and the first decades of the twentieth saw an explosion in science-fiction investigators. For example, Hesketh Vernon Hesketh-Prichard and his mother, Kate, writing under the pen names of E. and H. Heron, published a total of twelve stories in *Pearson's Magazine* featuring the protagonist Flaxman Low (1898–1899). One of the first fictional psychic detectives, Low possesses a thorough knowledge of the supernatural—he even reads "psychical periodicals" to keep up to date on ghostly happenings—as well as keen observational skills. Dr. John Silence, the "psychic doctor" created by the prolific ghost story and speculative fiction writer Algernon Blackwood, met immediate success when the collection *John Silence—Physician Extraordinary* was first published in 1908. Armed with both psychic sensitivity and scientific calm, the philanthropic physician Silence continues to be one of the most popular of the early science-fiction detectives.

William Hope Hodgson's Thomas Carnacki, Ghost Finder (1910–1948), is best remembered for his high-tech approach to investigations. He mixes contemporary technology (such as photography) with imaginary technology (such as his beloved "electric pentacle"), not unlike Walter's unique blend of scientific and science-fictional equipment in his lab. Sir Arthur Conan Doyle's other investigator besides Sherlock Holmes is a scientist: Professor George Edward Challenger, who appeared in four novels and two stories between 1912 and 1929. In *The Lost World* (1912), another character describes Challenger as "just a homicidal megalomaniac with a turn for science." Challenger certainly has a unique personality—often the proverbial rude, crude, and socially unacceptable—but he is also something of a scientific mastermind and jack-of-all trades, not unlike Walter. And like Walter and the rest of the science team, Challenger must uncover the truth behind a variety of fantastic phenomena, from possible apocalyptic scenarios that threaten the end of our world to new inventions that could prove dangerous in the wrong hands.

Perhaps one of the most original of the early science-fiction investigators is Andrew Latter, who appears in six short stories written by Harold Begbie and published in *London Magazine* in 1904. Latter becomes aware of a separate dreamland related to our Universe, and he visits there, finding clues to mysteries far closer to home. Latter's otherworldly travels anticipate the concept of astral projection, which Olivia identifies to Peter in the television series as a key component of fringe science. For that matter, the alternate dream reality shares similarities with *Fringe's* depiction of a parallel world similar to and yet different from our own. Latter's unique understanding of this realm and its secrets makes him an important consultant for Scotland Yard, much as Walter and Peter, both of whom have visited Over There, serve as important civilian consultants to the Fringe

Division. Latter's special access to this dreamworld makes him a valuable asset in solving crimes, much like Olivia's ability to travel back and forth between worlds and to identify artifacts from Over There makes her a valuable asset in conducting the Fringe Division's investigations.

Thus far, all of the early science-fiction investigators I've mentioned have been men. It's worth remembering that Olivia is the one in charge of the Fringe Division's science team. Does she have a literary predecessor? I nominate Shiela Crerar, Psychic Investigator, who appears in six stories by Ella Scrymsour across several 1920 issues of *The Blue Magazine*. When she approaches a case, Crerar employs traditional tools such as logic and compassion, but she also utilizes a very special gift: she can see ghosts. In a way, Crerar's psychic nature is similar to the cortex-iphan-altered Olivia's unique abilities both to travel to the alternate universe and to identify people and objects from Over There that now are in our world.

Crerar also shares another trait with Olivia: a hesitation to commit to romance. Throughout Scrymsour's short stories, Crerar finds herself the object of the dashing Stavordale Hartland's interest. She returns his affection and even requests his assistance in some of her work, but she postpones the idea of marriage in favor of pursuing her tasks as a detective. Some reviewers suggest that she seems to equate marriage with the end of her psychic abilities, as if she fears she might lose her powers along with her virginity.

Similarly, Olivia flounders in beginning and then consummating a relationship with Peter, despite strong mutual attraction. At least some of her misgivings relate to her gift—that is, her ability to see that Peter is from Over There, and the knowledge that her universe-hopping doppelganger has been together with Peter in her world. Despite complications in their personal lives, though, both Crerar and Olivia prove to be tireless in using their talents to investigate and solve fantastical mysteries.

Additional investigators from early science-fiction literature also deserve a place, if a more distant one, on branches of the *Fringe* family tree. These include J. Sheridan Le Fanu's Dr. Martin Hesselius and M.P. Shiel's Prince Zaleski from the nineteenth century, and Alice and Claude Askew's Aylmer Vance, Rose Champion de Crespigny's Norton Vise, and Seabury Quinn's Jules de Grandin in the early twentieth century, among others. All of these characters are committed to discovering the seemingly unknowable. By pioneering ahead into the great mysteries of the cosmos armed with both reason and imagination, they represent the curiosity and courage that fuel the scientific enterprise, even if, as in *Fringe*, some of their discoveries range far afield of reality as we understand it.

Televised Science-Fiction Investigators

Fringe is not the first television series to draw its inspiration from literary science-fiction investigators. In this sense, *Fringe* has a number of older siblings. Four trend-setting shows in particular stand out as forerunners to *Fringe* because of their popular success, uniqueness, and memorability. The first is a series of made-for-television serials by the BBC featuring the character of Professor Bernard Quatermass, a British scientist who investigates and combats sinister alien forces. The trilogy includes *The Quatermass Experiment* (1953), *Quatermass II* (1955), and *Quatermass and the Pit* (1958–1959). The BBC also brought Quatermass back to television in both 1979 and 2005. Quatermass has little of the ethical ambiguity of Walter in *Fringe* but much of Walter's genius, and his example confirms viewers' confidence in the power of science to provide solutions to our questions and protect us from the unknown.

Sapphire and Steel (1979–1982), a British series produced by ATV, focuses on cases in which time goes awry. The two title figures, Sapphire and Steel, are interdimensional operatives who investigate temporal problems and then restore the proper linear progression of events. Although they appear in human form, they possess superhuman powers. The mysterious Observers in *Fringe* share many traits with these cryptic characters, including an aloof perspective on humanity and an interest in a grand design or order that's beyond the knowledge of everyday human beings. *Sapphire and Steel* shares its trademark atmosphere of awe and disquiet, subtle horror, and wondering fear with *Fringe.*

In the United States, two popular series in particular anticipated *Fringe*. The first is *Kolchak: The Night Stalker*, which began as two made-for-television films in 1972 (*The Night Stalker*) and 1973 (*The Night Strangler*) and then ran as a series for the 1974–1975 season. A remake series briefly existed in 2005. Although he is a newspaper reporter instead of a scientist, Kolchak definitely counts as a science-fiction investigator. He specializes in researching and solving unusual crimes, many of which involve fantastical characters straight from the pages of classic genre literature, from androids and aliens to vampires and zombies. Like the Fringe Division's science team, Kolchak steps into the void left when traditional law enforcement will not or cannot pursue leads into the unknown.

The most successful television predecessor to *Fringe* is *The X-Files*, which ran from 1993–2002 and spawned two films (*The X-Files* in 1998 and *The X-Files: I Want to Believe* in 2008) and two spin-off series (*Millennium*, 1996–1999, and *The Lone Gunmen*, 2001). Fox Mulder and Dana Scully, similar to Olivia and Astrid in *Fringe*, are FBI agents whose investigations of bizarre cases lead them to make startling discoveries about our world and what lies beyond it. Like *Fringe*, *The X-Files* deals with areas of unorthodox science, intergenerational—at times inter-family—secrets, and potential threats to our planet. It's easy to see many of the classic science-fiction texts that inform *Fringe*, from works by Mary Wollstonecraft Shelley to H.P. Lovecraft, also mirrored in *The X-Files*.

Fringe departs most widely from its famous older sibling in the focus of its main arc; where *The X-Files* dwells on extrater-restrial life and the possible alien colonization of Earth, *Fringe* focuses on the alternate universe Over There and its pending retaliatory attack on our world. In both series, however, uneth-ical and unaccountable scientists are part of the problem, while rational and responsible science promises to provide our best chance at a solution. *The X-Files*' trademark slogan, "The truth is out there," confirms the same convictions that Walter and his companions profess, the basic tenants of science fiction itself: the Universe is comprehensible if approached rationally, and it's the very essence of human nature to seek to understand it.

Reanimation:
The H.P. Lovecraft Influence

With the exceptions of Mary Wollstonecraft Shelley, the writer of *Frankenstein*, and Edgar Allan Poe, the champion of ratiocination who set the stage for science-fiction investigators, no other author of early science fiction has left a greater imprint on *Fringe* than H.P. Lovecraft. A master of so-called "weird fiction," Lovecraft blended a distinctly modern form of cosmic horror with a science-fiction sensibility. Today, more than seventy years after his death, Lovecraft's work is more popular than ever, spawning film adaptations, games, music, artwork, countless pastiches, and even jewelry and perfume.

It's noteworthy that each of the concepts Olivia mentions in her description of fringe science—"mind control, teleportation, astral projection, invisibility, genetic mutation, reanimation" ("Pilot")—appear as plot elements in one or more stories by Lovecraft. For that matter, Olivia's explanation of The Pattern— "Inexplicable and frightening things are happening, and there's a connection somehow" ("The Same Old Story," 1-2)—could substitute as a synopsis for any number of Lovecraft's writings, or as a summary of his entire body of work as a whole.

Lovecraft's protagonists include intelligent and sensitive scholars, scientists, researchers, and medical men who genuinely want to uncover answers about the Universe around them. Often they become drawn into specific investigations due to their personal relationships or professional pursuits. Once on a case, they pursue it doggedly. What they discover horrifies them and sometimes costs them their sanity or their lives. In nearly every case, these investigators discover that humanity is small in a vast and impartial universe, and we are threatened by forces we can scarcely comprehend. Characters such as Professor Francis Wayland Thurston (*The Call of Cthulhu*, 1928), Professor William Dyer (*At the Mountains of Madness*, 1936), Dr. Elihu Whipple ("The Shunned House," 1937), and Dr. Marinus Bicknell (*The Case of Charles Dexter Ward*, 1941) are obvious ancestors of the members of the Fringe Division's science team.

The character most relevant to *Fringe*, however, is Lovecraft's own parody of Victor Frankenstein, the iconoclastic and unorthodox Dr. Herbert West of "Herbert West—Reanimator" (1922). Rather than create new life, West wishes to restore life to dead bodies, to "reanimate" them. At first blush, this sounds like a noble idea. To further his goal, however, he undertakes increasingly unethical research, progressing from grave robbery to murder in order to obtain specimens fresh enough for his experiments. Violent and zombie-like, the resulting reanimated corpses retain little of their original humanity. Like Victor before him and Walter after him, West ultimately suffers terrible repercussions for pursuing his scientific work with such intellectual arrogance and moral unaccountability. Thanks to "cult classic" films about Dr. Herbert West such as *Re-Animator* (1985), *Bride of Re-Animator* (1990), and *Beyond Re-Animator* (2003), fans of the genre have good reason to think immediately of Lovecraft's character whenever reanimation is mentioned.

Lovecraft's shadow looms large over *Fringe*. Lovecraft's beloved home town of Providence, Rhode Island, which often serves as a setting for his stories, also often serves as a setting for action in the television series. Perhaps the best example of *Fringe* acting as a love letter to Lovecraft can be found in the second-season episode

"Grey Matters." The episode is replete with tributes to Lovecraft's work: the administrator of one mental hospital is named Dr. West, as in the reanimator himself; another mental hospital visited by the team is Dunwich Mental Hospital, a reference to Lovecraft's story "The Dunwich Horror" (*Weird Tales*, 1829). A list of patients includes the names Joseph Slater (from Joe Slater in Lovecraft's "Beyond the Wall of Sleep"), Stuart Gordon (a filmmaker responsible for five movie/television adaptations of Lovecraft's works to date, including *Re-Animator*), and a woman named Crampton (a reference to "scream queen" actress Barbara Crampton, who has starred in three film adaptations of Lovecraft's stories, including *Re-Animator*).

This episode in particular led Goomi, the artist behind the long-running Lovecraft-based web comic *Unspeakable Vault (Of Doom)*, to pay homage to *Fringe* and its Lovecraftian flavor. The strip entitled "Vault 315: Fringe Division" depicts various characters created by Lovecraft, including the tentacled Cthulhu, ogling Olivia, who is identified by name. One notes, "Since the 90's, FBI agents are getting hotter!"

The Fox Network seems to appreciate the Lovecraft connection to *Fringe*, as well. During the third season of the show, Fox moved the series to the ever-unpopular Friday-night 9 P.M. Eastern time slot. Shortly before *Fringe* began airing on its new day and time on January 21, 2011, Fox ran "Friday Night Re-Animation" advertisements that made a joke about the scheduling change those "in the know" could recognize as Lovecraftian: "You may think Friday night is dead . . . but we're gonna re-animate it." Fortunately, the ad proved prophetic, and the series retained the ratings necessary to be renewed for a fourth season despite the scheduling shift.

The *Fringe* Family Tree

Each time I watch an episode of *Fringe*, I go into the experience with certain expectations of what I'll see. The characters will face something that's frightening, perhaps because it is beyond all human experience and explanation, or perhaps because it represents their personal pasts, their mistakes, and their frailties catching up with them. The setting of the episode, whether it's our world or the alternate one, might complicate my notions about who (if anyone) is heroic, and who (if anyone) is villainous. Walter will call Astrid by name—*a* name, but not *her* name. The science team members will try to wrestle the seemingly impossible into a form that's more understandable, and, if they are fortunate, the answers they uncover will outweigh the new questions they must ask. Faith in the power of science will remain unshaken, but faith in the all-too-human scientist will not.

Fringe undeniably delivers something new in television, but I am a fan of the series even more because it delivers something old: by asking what is possible, what is moral, and what is human, it distills the heart of the science-fiction tradition. When I look at Walter (or Walternate) and see echoes of Victor Frankenstein or Herbert West, and when I watch Olivia (or Fauxlivia) and see the reflection of Shiela Crerar, I appreciate how *Fringe* reimagines and engages with classic genre texts. In other words, I imagine that the literary ancestors of *Fringe* would be proud indeed of their twenty-first-century offspring.

➤ **AMY H. STURGIS** earned her PhD in intellectual history at Vanderbilt University. A specialist in science-fiction/ fantasy studies and Native American studies, Sturgis is the author of four books and the editor of another five. Her essays have appeared in dozens of scholarly journals, popular magazines, and books, including Smart Pop's *Nyx in the House of Night: Mythology, Folklore and Religion in the P.C. and Kristin Cast Vampyre Series* (2011). In 2006, she was honored with the Imperishable Flame Award for J.R.R. Tolkien Scholarship. In both 2009 and 2011, she received the Sofanaut Award for her regular "Looking Back at Genre History" segments on *StarShipSofa*, which in 2010 became the first podcast in history to win a Hugo Award. Her official website is amyhsturgis.com.

THE RETURN OF 1950s SCIENCE FICTION IN *FRINGE*

PAUL LEVINSON

There is a saying in Hollywood, "Steal from the best." Now the implementation of this is neither as cavalier nor as high-handed as perhaps initially it sounds: if you take a novel idea in another production that works particularly well, repackage that idea with your own unique spin, your creation should fare well. Clearly the creators of *Fringe* excel at this. Many of the sci-fi situations in *Fringe* have been done (sometimes done to death) previously, but the creators of the series excel at recycling, and putting their own unique spin on, sci-fi situations viewers have seen previously. Paul Levinson details for us the 1950s sci-fi concepts that have both clearly inspired, and been invoked by, the creative talent behind *Fringe*.

"There is nothing new under the sun"—from Ecclesiastes 1:9—is as true for our sun as for any alien sun, any sun in an alternate reality or a parallel universe, or even for a world, if one could exist, with no sun at all. Which is to say, that statement is as true for science fiction and its wondrous worlds as it is for our own world and lives. This does not mean that everything is trite or clichéd. If done right, the old in a new package can be especially exciting precisely *because* it evokes echoes of what we know. This is the secret of *Fringe*, whose stories are a compendium of highlights from the golden age of science fiction in the 1950s and shortly after.

There are times in history when certain cultural forms reach new heights—the play in the Elizabethan age, the poem in the Romantic era, and Impressionism in music, painting, and poetry at the end of the nineteenth century. The 1950s were such a time for science fiction. Spurred by wonder, awe, and trepidation about what science could do—the splitting of the atom, the launch of rockets, the discovery of DNA—the world of readers and viewers was hungry for treatment of scientific miracles, real and imagined, in fiction. A bevy of great science-fiction writers responded—not just Isaac Asimov, Robert Heinlein, and Arthur C. Clarke (known as the big three), but Alfred Bester, Daniel Keyes, Rod Serling, and many others—and created what we now call the golden age of science fiction. It was an age, published in pulp magazines or seen on black-and-white television in our living rooms and on silver screens in motion picture theaters, that *Fringe* was savvy to retrieve and reinvent.

By borrowing from this age, *Fringe* has been able to combine the dual appeal of being unexpected in its story lines—different from the science fiction around it, currently in our culture—yet comfortingly familiar. What follows are some of the 1950s elements that *Fringe* has taken up. These elements were not necessarily unique to science fiction in the 1950s golden age but were among the most popular and memorable themes from that era.

Surly Teleportation

If we could travel faster than the speed of sound in an aircraft—which became routine for pilots in the 1950s—why not travel instantaneously, at the speed of light, from one place to another?

Teleportation—the rough and grungy planet-bound kind, not the smooth, sparkly, outerspace "beaming" of *Star Trek*—rode high in the 1950s, due to Alfred Bester's novel *The Stars My Destination*. Published first as a series beginning in the October 1956 *Galaxy Magazine*, Bester's tale brought us the exploits of Gully Foyle, a futuristic *Count of Monte Cristo* character bent on revenge but with the capacity to "jaunte" or teleport over limited distances. The process is no pleasure and is fraught with risk, such as death if the teleporting person lacks a clear set of arrival coordinates.

Teleportation made its first major, ugly appearance in *Fringe* in "Safe" (1-10), an episode in which the criminal biochemist David Robert Jones is teleported from his super-high security prison in Frankfurt, Germany, to freedom in the United States—that is, he escaped from prison via teleportation, just as prisoners are wont to do in Gully Foyle's universe. We learn in "Ability" (1-14) that Jones used the "DizRay" device for teleportation, a technology that had been developed years earlier by Walter Bishop. As Walter explained, the teleportation process puts the mind and body through great trauma. Jones required two weeks in a decompression chamber after teleporting. As in *The Stars My Destination*, he or she who teleports in *Fringe* would be better off taking a plane or any other nonteleportation means of transport. The price of teleportation is too high to pay. This is clearly more realistic than the snap-your-fingers, almost Wizard-of-Oz transporter of *Star Trek*, where the device could certainly malfunction, but if it operated correctly, no harm came to the teleportees.

Indeed, so detrimental was *Fringe*'s teleportation to Jones that we learned in the season-one finale that its aftereffects were slowly killing him. He ultimately died when he was sliced in half in a last ill-fated teleportation effort, his body caught between our and the alternate universe. Teleportation on *Fringe* thus became part of its alternate reality story—which was only fitting, since cross-reality transport is certainly a super-kind of teleportation and subject to the same harsh physical effect on the transportees on *Fringe*.

Alternate Realities

Alternate realities, alternate histories, and parallel universes all pretty much amount to the same thing in science fiction: an alternate world that is somewhat the same and somewhat different from ours, another reality in which some of our events have already occurred, others have not, and still other events have occurred there that will never occur in our reality at all. We get a special intellectual kick—which taps into the "what if" of all science fiction ("what if" we could travel to another planet or galaxy or through time)—when we are coaxed to wonder what our world and lives would be like if just one little or big thing had happened differently in our history. One of the earliest and still best examples is Philip K. Dick's *The Man in the High Castle*, from the tail end of the golden age in 1962, now being made into a BBC miniseries by Ridley Scott. In a Second World War that ended in 1948, the Axis won and are now (in 1962) ensconced in the United States. *The Big Time* by Fritz Leiber, a short novel first published in two parts in the March and April 1958 issues of *Galaxy Magazine*, bears much less resemblance to our reality than *The Man in the High Castle*, but it features ongoing interaction between the two realities—in fact, a no-holds-barred war—which is another alternate-reality motif of *Fringe*.

Alternate realities became the dominant theme of *Fringe* in its season-one finale. (I like to think of this as *Fringe* finding itself in parallel worlds, in both meanings of the phrase "finding itself." The alternate universe appeared with little or no warning in the story, almost out of nowhere. And this literal turn of events finally put the series on firm footing—it found its "what-if" legs and the story it needed to tell.) The two realities became an underlying, frequent story line in season two, and often the only story told in season three. As I pointed out in an essay I wrote for *SciFiWire* just before the start of season two, a powerful scene in the season-one finale set in motion the central story for subsequent seasons: Walter stands by Peter's grave site in our reality. Peter apparently died as a child. But Peter has been very much alive in our reality. Ergo, Walter must have figured out a way, years ago, to go into the alternate reality and take its Peter back here to our reality, and raise alternate Peter as his own.

In seasons two and three, we learn that "Walternate"—Walter in the alternate reality—is bent on destroying our reality. He's motivated by personal fury over the kidnapping of his son and his professional view that only one of the two realities can survive in the long run. This Walter is more ruthless and less cracked than our Walter, and possibly more intelligent, since our Walter had his friend and colleague William Bell remove parts of his brain (which would also account for at least part of our Walter's crackage).

But differences between alternate realities are especially effective when the differences are about real events already known by most readers or viewers, such as Germany not losing but winning World War II in *The Man in the High Castle*. Among the most appealing ways in which the alternate reality differs from ours in *Fringe* are similar historical details (which may or may not be connected to our story's motivating event): JFK was not assassinated and is still alive. The World Trade Center towers are still standing; in the parallel world, the attack on September 11, 2001, took out the White House, which is currently being rebuilt with Obama in the presidency. This brings home a key ingredient in the most successful alternate reality stories: don't make too much different; keep some prominent aspects the same, because that makes the differences all the more chilling. It's almost our reality, but not, shockingly, quite. In Robert Harris' 1992 *Fatherland*, another, much later take on *The Man in the High Castle* and the Nazis winning the war, this is accomplished by the success of "Das Beatles" in this alternate Germanic current world. We get the same chill when we see their posters hanging on the streets of alternate Germany that we do when we see the dirigibles in the sky over New York City's familiar skyline in *Fringe*'s alternate reality.

The presence of the dirigibles suggests they are still a major way of flying, which means there likely were no R101 and Hindenburg disasters there either—no "oh, the humanity!"— which spelled the end of dirigibles for commercial air flight over here in our reality. But the other side is by no means all sun and light in comparison to ours. Indeed, the alternate reality has suffered far more than ours from Walter's well-meaning burglary of a son—after all, because he brought alternate Peter here, he was able to cure him—and has led to not only Walternate but Fauxlivia being more ruthless (and in Walternate's case, more grim) than our Walter and Olivia.

Mole People in *Fringe*

Aside from teleportation and alternate reality, much of the content in *Fringe* in the past three seasons has been brutal, shocking, often verging on horror or the science-fiction sector of the horror narrative genre. This has been a staple of science fiction since the early 1900s but was especially well represented in the 1950s golden age, in which movies such as *Them*, *The Blob*, *The Fly*, and *The Mole People* were major events for teenagers in drive-in theaters.

The idea of people living underground, posing some kind of real or potential threat to people living on the surface, first came into the popular culture spotlight with the Morlocks in H.G. Wells' *The Time Machine* in 1895. The Morlocks were pale, ugly to the point of grotesque, and, unsurprisingly, no fans of sunlight. They had the characteristics of subterranean dwellers we would encounter in later science fiction, but they were only a part of the Wells story.

People beneath the Earth took center stage in the 1956 movie *The Mole People*, directed by Virgil W. Vogel. They got there when their ancestors headed down in response to ancient floods in Mesopotamia. How and why the people beneath the Earth came to be there is always a major part of the subterranean story. In the original *Time Machine*, the Morlocks are the descendants of the human working class, giving Wells a chance to employ them for his social commentary on the mistreatment of laborers. In later movie remakes, the Morlocks are humans who headed down for safety during apocalyptic wars, as people in London actually did when they went to the "underground"—subways—to seek shelter from German air attacks in the Second World War.

Rather than using it as social commentary, *Fringe* in "Night of Desirable Objects" (2-2) came up with a more personal, individualistic rendition of this story. A scientist impregnated his wife, who had lupus. This would ordinarily have prevented her from coming to term, because the immune disorder underlying lupus would have destroyed the fetus. So the scientist put scorpion and mole-rat DNA into the embryo to increase its resiliency. The mother still died. The baby apparently died. But it actually dug its way out of the little casket and proceeded to take up residence underground, from where it eventually arose to take on Olivia and Peter.

Although the story has thus far not been a continuing one on *Fringe*, it epitomizes *Fringe*'s continuing connection to the grade-B horror movie and its perennial appeal: for whatever reason, many of us enjoy being unsettled, frightened, and even slightly revolted by what we see on the screen.

Beguiled Eye of the Beholder

Fringe is not a pretty series. This is no doubt deliberate because, as indicated above, there can be an appeal in the physically off-putting, in images that make us squirm. *Fringe*'s tech is rarely sleek and shiny and is usually evocative of Victorian steam punk, dark and groaning. This grit is one of the unspoken foundations of the series—a pervasive backdrop that is rarely if ever remarked upon by the characters. But if the repulsive can be attractive, can coax us to watch more rather than turn away, this raises the deep, aesthetic question of what, really, is beauty? *Fringe* tackles this issue head-on in "Johari Window" (2-12), with a consideration of what is beautiful, what is ugly, and why.

The golden age predecessor of this story is one of the most celebrated episodes of *The Twilight Zone* television series—and justly so—from November 1960, "The Eye of the Beholder" (2-6). A woman in a hospital is desperate for an operation to improve her looks. Everyone who sees her is clearly repulsed. She receives the operation, but when the bandages come off her face, we discover from the reactions of the medical staff that the operation didn't work—she'll have to go live with people of her own kind, who won't be traumatized by her condition. But in the very last scene, we get a glimpse of the patient's face: she's beautiful (by our, the viewers', standards), and the medical staff all have pig faces.

"Johari Window" offered its own take on this now classic story.

A US Army project from decades ago tried to make soldiers invisible by scrambling the optic nerves of all who saw them. The experiment failed and also disfigured all the inhabitants of the town where the research was conducted. The chief scientist did his best to counter this result: he created an electromagnetic pulse that fooled the eyes of everyone who lived in the town, as well as everyone who visited the town, into not seeing the inhabitants as disfigured. (This gambit was also the crux of the pilot of the original *Star Trek* television series—later broadcast as the two-part episode "The Menagerie" [1-11 and 1-12]—in which the inhabitants of a planet make the disfigured Captain Pike and his lover look beautiful in each other's eyes.)

Flowers for *Fringenon*

Remedies for inadequacies, whether physical or mental, whether caused by humans interfering with nature or arising from nature itself, have also been a stock-in-trade of science fiction for many years. The key part of such stories is usually the effectiveness of the remedy, the price we have to pay for it, and its impact on other aspects of our lives. This was the theme of one of the most widely read science-fiction stories of all time: "Flowers for Algernon" by Daniel Keyes, first published in *The Magazine of Fantasy & Science Fiction* in April 1959, later expanded and published as a novel, and since read in junior high school and high school classes all over the world (see Wikipedia for various references).

In "Flowers for Algernon," the mouse named in the title is operated upon and made highly intelligent. This encourages the scientist to operate upon Charley, a man, who is transformed from mentally retarded to genius. But the mouse begins to regress, and in the heartbreaking denouement of the story, Charley realizes he will go the same way. We then watch as his mental capacities indeed deteriorate.

As Walter's character and history emerged and developed after the first season of *Fringe*, a related theme became a central feature of his ongoing narrative. Why is our Walter somewhat crazy, rendering him into the quintessential mad scientist? We learn in "Over There (Part 2)" (2-23) that Walter asked William Bell to take out parts of Walter's brain. We discover in subsequent episodes that Walter wanted this because he was afraid his extraordinary intelligence could do untold damage to the two universes. By "Reciprocity" (3-11), however, Walter has reversed his opinion, now wanting to reattain his lost brain power to better counter Walternate and protect Peter. Fortunately, Bell left a serum at Massive Dynamic in our reality that could stimulate the growth of Walter's brain cells and restore the missing pieces. As of the end of that episode, Walter had only managed to attain some temporary chimplike characteristics, rather than his original brain function, since the unlabeled serum he took was intended for chimpanzee, not human, brain cell regeneration.

In "The Last Sam Weiss" (3-21), Walter told Olivia that he's come to terms with his lost intelligence, and even thinks it may have made him the unique thinker that he is now. But the human serum remains at Massive Dynamic somewhere, and so the "Flowers for *Fringe*non" question remains open. If Walter were to reverse his opinion on this matter and take this serum, would it indeed bring back his full intelligence? If so, with what consequence for Walter and everyone else? And would the effects be

permanent, or, like Algernon and Charley, only tragically temporary? Since Walter, unlike Algernon and Charley, was highly
intelligent in the first place—and thus the serum would be
restorative for Walter, rather than additive like the Algernon
surgery—there is perhaps more hope for Walter (if not necessarily for the rest of the world, since we do not yet know what
impact a Walter with heightened intelligence will have).

Sound that Kills

For Walter, his restored intelligence would be one of the best
weapons he could muster. *Fringe*, as befits a neo-classic retro
science-fiction series, exalts in all manner of unconventional
weaponry, including what can be done with sound.

In the aftermath of the atom bomb and the V-2 rocket, science
fiction in the 1950s paid special attention to all sorts of scientifically plausible if not yet possible weapons. Some were highly
personal and targeted victims on a one-by-one basis.

Science Fiction Theater—an anthology series of stand-alone
episodes—ran for two years on American television, 1955–1957,
and paved the way for *The Twilight Zone*. Its stories became a
source book for later science fiction.

Fringe picked up a sound theme from the final episode of
Science Fiction Theater, which aired in April 1957. It was entitled
"The Sound that Kills" (2-39) and featured a spy who murdered
inconvenient people by sound—which could conveniently be sent
through the telephone. You pick up a ringing phone, put it to your
ear, and your assassin slays you with a deadly burst of frequency
and amplitude. In "The Box" (3-2), *Fringe* introduced a similar

device, a box that emitted lethal ultrasonic frequencies. And there was a nice twist: an intended victim survived because he was deaf. Alas, he was later killed the old-fashioned way, with bullets from Fauxlivia's gun, but the acoustic point was still well made.

It's worth noting that *Fringe* has another kind of connection to the *Science Fiction Theater* anthology show. In the first season, *Fringe* was in many ways closer to a science-fiction anthology than a continuing drama with an unfolding story. Although the leading characters were the same (and Walter's story was always intended to come to the fore eventually), the stories bore little or no connection to one another, less even than we might see in generally stand-alone episodes of such procedural shows as *NCIS* and *Criminal Minds*. But anthologies are difficult sells, at least in today's television environment, and *Fringe* wisely pivoted into a much more continuing story at the end of season one, as we already saw. This is almost certainly why *Fringe* lasted at least three seasons and has been renewed for a fourth, in contrast to the two seasons of *Science Fiction Theater*—viewers prefer a show they can follow week to week, with characters they can grow to care about, rather than a string of self-contained narratives.

The Monster Next Door

Whether in *The Twilight Zone* episode "The Monsters Are Due on Maple Street" (1-22) from 1960—where the people next door are not monsters, only people their neighbors are manipulated by aliens to think are monsters—or in Zenna Henderson's "The People" stories published in the 1950s—where the humanoids among us really are aliens, trying to live here quietly and in peace—the notion that your next-door neighbor, or the guy behind the counter in your local candy store, can be someone profoundly alien and potentially dangerous has shown up often in science fiction. The notion is irresistible because, let's face it, we've all wondered at some time or another in our lives if the person ahead of us in line in a supermarket or a convenience store came from outer space.

Fringe of course couldn't resist playing with this classic sci-fi concept and brought us Sam Weiss in "Night of Desirable Objects," the same episode that presented *Fringe*'s version of *The Mole People*. Sam worked in a bowling alley—you can't get much more next-door than that—but he had special knowledge helpful to Olivia in navigating her mind and world. In "Concentrate and Ask Again" (3-12) Nina discovered that he was the author of *The First People*, a book that we until then were led to think was written by some forgotten ancient or prehistoric people (another classic science-fiction theme). Since the book is about the construction of the super, apocalyptic weapon that Walternate is apparently trying to program Peter to use to destroy our world, Sam's role in this was no small matter. He went on in "6:02 A.M. EST" (3-20) and "The Last Sam Weiss" to help Olivia discover her crucial role in disarming the doomsday machine that Walternate had set in motion.

Though monsters living next door don't abound in *Fringe*, they play important roles in stories other than Sam's. The shapeshifters are literally monsters, waiting to be activated to do their damage. The bald Observers live outside our timeline, but they pass us on the streets and are always on the sidelines in one place or another. And even Fauxlivia, beautiful as she is, could be considered a monstrous version of Olivia—certainly Olivia thinks so—and she lived worse than next door to Peter, sharing his very bed.

• • •

And that, in a nutshell, is what's so original about *Fringe*. That's the signpost up ahead. There's nothing wrong with your television set. No aliens in ships in the sky, no whirling time machines, just little things harvested from the cream of the crop of golden age science fiction, blended together to give us reality-shattering consequences. *Fringe* has succeeded by taking stories that some of us are so familiar with that we took for granted (and that some viewers had forgotten and still others never knew in the first place), recognizing their timeless appeal, and dressing them up in twenty-first-century clothing. The result is a science-fiction series not just from the golden age but for the ages.

PAUL LEVINSON, PHD, is Professor of Communication & Media Studies at Fordham University in NYC. His nonfiction books, including *The Soft Edge* (1997), *Digital McLuhan* (1999), *Realspace* (2003), *Cellphone* (2004), and *New New Media* (2009), have been translated into ten languages. His science-fiction novels include *The Silk Code* (1999), *Borrowed Tides* (2001), *The Consciousness Plague* (2002), *The Pixel Eye* (2003), and *The Plot To Save Socrates* (2006). He appears on *The O'Reilly Factor* and numerous TV and radio programs. His 1972 LP, *Twice Upon a Rhyme*, was reissued in 2010. He reviews television in his InfiniteRegress.tv blog, and was listed in *The Chronicle of Higher Education*'s Top 10 Academic Twitterers in 2009.

PARALLEL UNIVERSES

MAX TEGMARK

In different forms parallel universes have been a fixture in science-fiction literature, cinema, and TV since the early days of the genre. Modern research suggests that the notion of a realm "parallel" to our own isn't merely a storyteller's device. It turns out that there may actually be theoretical and experimental bases for believing that parallel universes and alternate realities exist. In our reality MIT theoretical physicist Max Tegmark, PhD, makes the case for alternity.

NOTE: *The following reprinted piece is adapted from Max Tegmark's longer article "Parallel Universes," which discusses four levels of multiple universes rather than the three included here. You can read the full version online at his website, at http://space.mit.edu/home/tegmark/crazy.html.*

I s there another copy of you reading this article, deciding to put it aside without finishing this sentence while you are reading on? A person living on a planet called Earth, with misty mountains, fertile fields, and sprawling cities, in a solar system with seven other planets? The life of this person has been identical to yours in every respect—until now, that is, when your decision to read on signals that your two lives are diverging.

You probably find this idea strange and implausible, and I must confess that this is my gut reaction, too. Yet it looks like we will just have to live with it, since the simplest and most popular cosmological model today predicts that this person actually exists in a galaxy about 10^{29} meters from here. This does not even assume speculative modern physics, merely that space is infinite and rather uniformly filled with matter. Your *alter ego* is simply a prediction of the concordance model of cosmology, which agrees with all current observational evidence and is used as the basis for most calculations and simulations presented at cosmology conferences. In contrast, alternative cosmological models, such as a fractal universe, a closed universe, and a multiply connected universe, have been seriously challenged by observations.

The farthest you can observe is the distance that light has been able to travel during the 14 billion years since the Big-Bang expansion began. The most distant visible objects are now about 4×10^{26} meters away, and a sphere of this radius defines our observable Universe, also called our *Hubble volume*, our *horizon volume*, or simply our Universe. Likewise, the universe of your above-mentioned twin is a sphere of the same size centered beyond our Universe, none of which we can see or have any causal contact with yet. This is the simplest (but far from the only) example of parallel universes.

By this very definition of "universe" one might expect the notion that our observable Universe is merely a small part of a larger "multiverse" to be forever in the domain of metaphysics. Yet the epistemological border between physics and metaphysics is defined by whether a theory is experimentally testable, not by whether it is weird or involves unobservable entities. The frontiers of physics have gradually expanded to incorporate ever more abstract (and once metaphysical) concepts such as a round, rotating Earth, invisible electromagnetic fields, time slowdown

FIGURE 1

LEVEL 1:
Regions Beyond Our Cosmic Horizon
FEATURES:
Same laws of physics, different conditions
ASSUMPTIONS:
Infinite space, ergodic matter distribution
EVIDENCE:
Microwave background measurements point to flat, infinite space, large-scale smoothness; Simplest model

LEVEL 2:
Other Post-Inflation Bubbles
FEATURES:
Same fundamental equations of physics, but perhaps different constants, particles, and dimensionality
ASSUMPTION:
Chaotic inflation occurred
EVIDENCE:
Inflation theory explains flat space, scale-invariant fluctuations, solves horizon problem and monopole problems, and can naturally explain such bubbles; Explains fine-tuned parameters

LEVEL 3:
The Many Worlds of Quantum Physics
FEATURES:
Same as level 2
ASSUMPTION:
Physics unitary
EVIDENCE:
Experimental support for unitary physics; AdS/CFT correspondence suggests that even quantum gravity is unitary; Decoherence experimentally verified; Mathematically simplest model

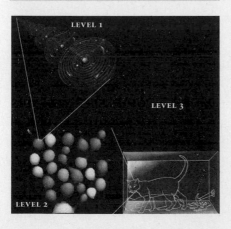

at high speeds, quantum superpositions, curved space, and black holes. The concept of a multiverse has joined this list. It is becoming increasingly clear that multiverse models grounded in modern physics can, in fact, be empirically testable, predictive, and falsifiable. Indeed, as many as four distinct types of parallel universes (Figure 1) are discussed in the recent scientific literature, so that the key question is not whether there is a multiverse, but rather how many levels it has.

I. Level I: Regions Beyond Our Cosmic Horizon

Let us return to your distant twin. If space is infinite and the distribution of matter sufficiently uniform on large scales, then even the most unlikely events must occur somewhere. In particular, there are infinitely many other inhabited planets, including infinitely many people with the same appearance, name, and memories as you. Indeed, there are infinitely many other regions the size of our observable Universe, where every possible history is played out. This is the Level I multiverse.

A. Evidence for Level I Parallel Universes

Though the implications may seem counterintuitive, this spatially infinite cosmological model is in fact the simplest and most popular one among physicists today. It is part of the cosmological concordance model, which agrees with all current observational evidence and is used as the basis for most calculations and simulations presented at cosmology conferences. Alternately, models such as a fractal universe, a closed universe, and a multiply connected universe have been seriously challenged by observations. Yet the Level I multiverse idea has been controversial in the past, so let us review the status of its two underlying assumptions (infinite space and "sufficiently uniform" distribution).

How large is space? Observationally, the lower bound has grown dramatically with no indication of an upper bound. We accept the existence of things that we cannot see but could see if we moved or waited, like ships beyond the horizon. Objects beyond the cosmic horizon have similar status, since the observable Universe grows by a light-year every year as light from farther away reaches us. Since we all learn about simple Euclidean space in school, it can be difficult to imagine how space could *not* be infinite—for what would lie beyond the sign saying *"SPACE ENDS HERE—MIND THE GAP"*? Einstein's theory of gravity allows space to be finite by being differently connected than Euclidean space, say with the topology of a four-dimensional sphere or a doughnut so that traveling far in one direction brings you back from the opposite direction. In addition, a spatially infinite universe is a prediction of the cosmological theory of inflation (Garriga & Vilenkin 2001b). The striking successes of inflation therefore lends further support to the idea that space is simple and infinite just as we learned in school.

INFLATION: a theory of cosmology that suggests the nature of the observable universe can be explained by the universe's rapid expansion after the Big Bang

How uniformly is matter distributed on large scales? In an "island universe" model where space is infinite but all the matter is confined to a finite region, almost all members of the Level I multiverse would be practically empty space. Another nonuniform alternative is a fractal universe, where the matter distribution is self-similar and all coherent structures in the galaxy distribution are a small part of even larger coherent structures larger than about 1024m. The island and fractal universe models have both been demolished by recent observations, however. Maps of the three-dimensional galaxy distribution have shown that the spectacular large-scale structure, when observed, gives way to dull uniformity on large scales, with no large coherent structures. The Sloan Digital Sky Survey and cosmic microwave background (CMB) measurements have established that the trend toward uniformity continues all the way out to the edge of our observable Universe.

The observations thus speak loud and clear: space as we know it continues far beyond the edge of our observable Universe, and is teeming with galaxies.

B. What Are Level I Parallel Universes Like?

The physics description of the world is traditionally split into two parts: initial conditions and laws of physics specifying how the initial conditions evolve. Observers living in parallel universes at Level I observe the exact same laws of physics as we do, but with different initial conditions than those in our Hubble volume. The currently favored theory is that the initial conditions (the densities and motions of matter early on) were created by quantum fluctuations during the inflation epoch (see section

3). This quantum mechanism generates initial conditions that are essentially random, producing density fluctuations described by what mathematicians call an ergodic random field. *Ergodic* means that if you generate an ensemble of universes, each with its own random initial conditions, then the probability distribution of outcomes in a given volume is identical to the distribution that you get by sampling different volumes in a single universe. In other words, everything that could in principle have happened here did in fact happen elsewhere.

 INITIAL CONDITIONS: the ground rules of a system; in this case, the laws of physics in our Universe

Inflation generates all possible initial conditions with non-zero probability, the most likely initial conditions being almost uniform with fluctuations that are amplified by gravitational clustering to form galaxies, stars, planets, and other structures. This means that nearly all imaginable matter configurations occur in some Hubble volume far away, and also that we should expect our own Hubble volume to be fairly typical—at least typical among those that contain observers.

This raises an interesting philosophical point that will come back and haunt us in Section IVB: if there are indeed many copies of "you" with identical past lives and memories, you would not be able to compute your own future even if you had complete knowledge of the entire state of the cosmos! The reason is that there is no way for you to determine which of these copies is "you" (they all feel that they are). Yet their lives will typically begin to differ eventually, so the best you can do is predict probabilities for what you will experience from now on. This kills the notion of determinism.

C. How a Multiverse Theory Can Be Tested and Falsified

Is a multiverse theory one of metaphysics rather than physics? The distinction between the two is whether the theory is empirically testable and falsifiable. Containing unobservable entities clearly does *not* per se make a theory nontestable. For instance, a theory stating that there are 666 parallel universes, all of which are devoid of oxygen, makes the testable prediction that we should observe no oxygen here, and is therefore ruled out by observation.

As a more serious example, the Level I multiverse framework is routinely used to rule out theories in modern cosmology, although this is rarely spelled out explicitly. For instance, CMB observations have recently shown that space has almost no curvature. Hot and cold spots in CMB maps have a characteristic size that depends upon the curvature of space, and the observed spots appear too large to be consistent with the previously popular "open universe" model.

However, the average spot size randomly varies slightly from one Hubble volume to another, so it is important to be statistically rigorous. When cosmologists say that the open universe model is ruled out at 99.9 percent confidence, they really mean that if the open universe model were true, then fewer than one out of every thousand Hubble volumes would show CMB spots as large as those we observe—therefore the entire model with all its infinitely many Hubble volumes is ruled out, even though we have of course only mapped the CMB in our own particular Hubble volume.

The lesson to learn from this example is that multiverse theories *can* be tested and falsified, but only if they predict what the ensemble of parallel universes is and specify a probability distribution (or more generally what mathematicians call a *measure*) over it. As we will see in Section IVB, this measure problem can be quite serious and is still unsolved for some multiverse theories.

II. Level II: Other Postinflation Bubbles

If you felt that the Level I multiverse was hard to stomach, try imagining an infinite set of distinct ones (each symbolized by a bubble in Figure 1), some perhaps with different dimensionality and physical constants. This is what is predicted by the popular chaotic theory of inflation, and we refer to it as the Level II multiverse. These other domains are more than infinitely far away, in the sense that you would never get there even if you traveled at the speed of light forever. The reason is that the space between our Level I multiverse and its neighbors is still undergoing inflation, which keeps stretching it out and creating more volume faster than you can travel through it. In contrast, you could travel to an arbitrarily distant Level I universe if you were patient and cosmic expansion decelerates.

A. Evidence for Level II Parallel Universes

The Big Bang model proved a highly successful explanation of most of the history of our Universe. It explained how a primordial fireball expanded and cooled, synthesized helium during the first few minutes, became transparent after 400,000 years releasing the cosmic microwave background radiation, and gradually got clumpier due to gravitational clustering. Still, disturbing questions remained about what happened in the very beginning. Did something appear from nothing? Why is space so big, so old, and so flat, when generic initial conditions predict curvature to grow over time and the density to approach either zero or infinity? What mechanism generated the gravitational fluctuations out of which all structure grew?

A process known as *inflation* solves all these problems in one fell swoop, and has emerged as the most popular theory of what happened very early on. Inflation suggests that space is flat and uniform but stretching rapidly, like the surface of an expanding balloon. As space stretches, quantum vacuum fluctuations stretch as well, into macroscopically large density fluctuations that seed galaxy formation.

In the popular model known as *chaotic inflation*, inflation ends in some regions of space allowing life as we know it, whereas quantum fluctuations cause other regions of space to inflate even faster. In essence, one inflating bubble sprouts other inflationary bubbles, which in turn produce others in a never-ending chain reaction (Figure 1, lower left, with time increasing upwards). The bubbles where inflation has ended are the elements of the Level II multiverse.

Each such bubble is infinite in size, yet there are infinitely many bubbles since the chain reaction never ends. If this exponential growth of the number of bubbles has been going on forever, there will be an infinity of such parallel universes. In this case, there is also no beginning of time and no absolute Big Bang: there is, was, and always will be an infinite number of inflating bubbles and postinflationary regions, forming a fractal pattern.

B. What Are Level II Parallel Universes Like?

The prevailing view is that the physics we observe today is merely a low-energy limit of a much more symmetric theory that manifests itself at extremely high temperatures. This underlying fundamental theory may be eleven-dimensional, supersymmetric, and involving a grand unification of the four fundamental forces of nature. A common feature in such theories is that the potential energy of the field(s) driving inflation has several different minima (sometimes called "vacuum states"), corresponding to different ways of breaking this symmetry and, as a result, to different low-energy physics. For instance, all but three spatial dimensions could be curled up, resulting in an effectively three-dimensional space like ours, or fewer could curl up, leaving a seven-dimensional space. The quantum fluctuations driving chaotic inflation could cause different symmetry breaking in different bubbles, resulting in different members of the Level II multiverse having different dimensionality. Many symmetries observed in particle physics also result from the specific way in which symmetry is broken, so there could be Level II parallel universes where there are, say, two rather than three generations of quarks.

In addition to such discrete properties as dimensionality and fundamental particles, our Universe is characterized by a set of dimensionless numbers known as *physical constants*. Examples include the electron/proton mass ratio mp/me≈ 1836 and the cosmological constant, which appears to be about 10^{-123} in so-called Planck units. There are also models where such continuous parameters can vary from one post-inflationary bubble to another. The Level II multiverse is therefore likely to be more diverse than the Level I multiverse, containing domains where not only the initial conditions differ, but perhaps the dimensionality, the elementary particles, and the physical constants differ as well.

If one Level II multiverse can exist, eternally self-reproducing in a fractal pattern, then there may well be infinitely many other completely disconnected Level II multiverses. However, this variant appears to be untestable, since it would neither add any qualitatively different worlds nor alter the probability distribution for their properties. All possible initial conditions and symmetry breakings are already realized within each one. An idea proposed by Tolman andWheeler and recently elaborated by Steinhardt & Turok (2002) is that the (Level I) multiverse is cyclic, going through an infinite series of Big Bangs. If it exists, the ensemble of such incarnations would also form a multiverse, arguably with a diversity similar to that of Level II.

According to yet another idea, the braneworld scenario, an additional three-dimensional world could be quite literally parallel to ours, merely offset in a higher dimension. However, it is unclear whether such a world (or "brane") deserves to be called a parallel universe separate from our own, since we may be able to interact with it gravitationally, much as we do with dark matter.

C. Fine-Tuning and Selection Effects

Physicists dislike unexplained coincidences. Indeed, they interpret them as evidence that models are ruled out.

Suppose you check into a hotel, are assigned room 1967 and, surprised, note that this is the year you were born. After a moment of reflection, you conclude that this is not that surprising after all, given that the hotel has many rooms and that you would not be having these thoughts in the first place if you'd been assigned another one. You then realize that even if you knew nothing about hotels, you could have inferred the existence of other hotel rooms from just the number on this one, because if there were only one room number in the entire Universe, you would be left with an unexplained coincidence.

Although the existence of other hotel rooms is uncontroversial and observationally confirmed, that of parallel universes is not, since they cannot be observed. Yet if fine-tuning is observed in our Universe, one can argue for the existence of parallel universes using the exact same logic as above. Indeed, there are numerous examples of fine-tuning suggesting parallel universes with other physical constants, although the degree of fine-tuning is still under active debate and should be clarified by additional calculations.

 FINE-TUNING: the idea, in physics, that if some physical parameters were slightly changed, our Universe would not exist

For instance, if the electromagnetic force were weakened by a mere 4 percent, then the sun would immediately explode. If it were stronger, there would be fewer stable atoms. Indeed, most if not all the parameters affecting low-energy physics appear fine-tuned at some level, in the sense that changing them by modest amounts results in a qualitatively different universe. If the weak interaction (between elementary particles) were substantially weaker, there would be no hydrogen around, since it would have been converted to helium shortly after the Big Bang. If the protons were 0.2 percent heavier, they would decay into neutrons unable to hold onto electrons, so there would be no stable atoms. If the proton/electron mass ratio were much smaller, there could be no stable stars, and if it were much larger, there could be no ordered structures like crystals and DNA molecules.

The standard model of particle physics has twenty-eight free parameters, and cosmology may introduce additional independent ones. If we really do live in a Level II multiverse, then for those parameters that vary between the parallel universes, we will never be able to predict our measured values from first principles. We can merely compute probability distributions for what we should expect to find, taking selection effects into account. We should expect to find everything that can vary across the ensemble to be as generic as is consistent with our existence. However, as detailed in Section IVB, this issue of what is "generic" and, more specifically, how to compute probabilities in physics, is emerging as an embarrassingly thorny problem.

III. Level III: The Many Worlds of Quantum Physics

There may be a third type of parallel worlds that are not far away but are in a sense right here. If the fundamental equations of physics are what mathematicians call *unitary*, as they so far appear to be, then the Universe keeps branching into parallel universes as in the cartoon (Figure 2, bottom): whenever a quantum event appears to have a random outcome, all outcomes in fact occur, one in each branch. This is the Level III multiverse. Although more debated and controversial than Level I and Level II, we will see that, surprisingly, this level adds no new types of universes.

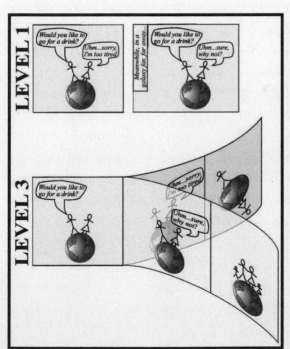

FIGURE 2: Difference between Level I and Level III. Whereas Level I parallel universes are far away in space, those of Level III are right here, with quantum events causing classical reality to split and diverge into parallel story lines. Yet Level III adds no new story lines beyond levels I or II.

A. Evidence for Level III Parallel Universes

Early last century, the theory of quantum mechanics revolution-
ized physics by explaining the atomic realm. Despite the obvious
successes in its application (chemistry, nuclear reactions, LASERs,
semiconductors), an ongoing heated debate ensued about its
interpretation. In quantum theory, the state of the Universe is not
given in classical terms such as the positions and velocities of all
particles, but by a mathematical abstraction called a wave function. According to the Schrödinger equation, this state evolves
deterministically over time in a fashion termed *unitary*. The
sticky part is that there are perfectly legitimate wave functions
corresponding to classically counterintuitive situations such as
you being in two different places at once. Worse, the Schrödinger
equation can evolve innocent classical states into schizophrenic
ones. As a baroque example, Schrödinger described the famous
thought experiment where a nasty contraption kills a cat if a
radioactive atom decays. Since the radioactive atom eventually
enters a superposition of decayed and not decayed, it produces a
cat that is both dead and alive.

In the 1920s, this weirdness was explained away by postu-
lating that the wave function "collapsed" into some definite
classical outcome whenever an observation was made, with
specific outcome probabilities given by the wave function.
Einstein was unhappy about such intrinsic randomness in
nature, which violated unitarity, insisting that "God doesn't
play dice." Others complained that there was no equation specifying when this collapse occurred. In his PhD thesis, Princ-
eton student Hugh Everett III showed that this controversial
collapse postulate was unnecessary. Quantum theory predicted

that one classical reality would gradually split into superpositions of many (Figure 2). He showed that observers would subjectively experience this splitting merely as a slight randomness, and indeed with probabilities in exact agreement with those from the old collapse postulate. This superposition of classical worlds is the Level III multiverse.

Everett's work had left two crucial questions unanswered: First, if the world actually contains bizarre macrosuperpositions, then why don't we perceive them? The answer came in 1970, when Dieter Zeh showed that the Schrödinger equation itself gives rise to a type of censorship effect. This effect became known as *decoherence*, and was worked out in great detail over the following decades. Coherent quantum superpositions were found to persist only as long as they were kept secret from the rest of the world. A single collision with a snooping photon or air molecule is sufficient to ensure that our friends in Figure 2 can never be aware of their counterparts in the parallel story line. A second unanswered question in the Everett picture was subtle but equally important: what physical mechanism picks out approximately classical states (e.g., states where an object is in only one place, etc.) as special? Decoherence answered this question as well, showing that classical states are simply those that are most robust against decoherence. In summary, decoherence both identifies Level III parallel universes and delimits them from one another. Decoherence is now quite uncontroversial and has been experimentally measured in a wide range of circumstances. Since decoherence mimics wave function collapse, it has eliminated much of the original motivation for nonunitary quantum mechanics and made Everett's many worlds interpretation increasingly popular.

> **DECOHERENCE:** the appearance that the physical possibilities have been reduced into a single possibility when seen by an observer

If the time-evolution of the wave function is unitary, then the Level III multiverse exists, so physicists have worked hard on testing this crucial assumption. No departures from unitarity have been found yet. In the last few decades, remarkable experiments have confirmed unitarity for ever larger systems. A leading argument against unitarity has involved destruction of information during the evaporation of black holes, suggesting that quantum-gravitational effects are nonunitary and collapse the wave function. However, a recent string theory breakthrough has suggested that even quantum gravity is unitary.

> **TIME-EVOLUTION:** the change of state brought about by the passage of time

B. What Are Level III Parallel Universes Like?

When discussing parallel universes, we need to distinguish between two different ways of viewing a physical theory: the outside view or *bird perspective* of a mathematician studying its mathematical underpinnings, and the inside view or *frog perspective* of an observer living in the world described by the equations. From the bird perspective, the Level III multiverse is simple:

there is only one wave function, and it evolves smoothly and deterministically over time without any sort of splitting or parallelism. The abstract quantum world described by this evolving wave function contains within it a vast number of parallel classical storylines (Figure 2), continuously splitting and merging, as well as a number of quantum phenomena that lack a classical description. From her frog perspective, however, each observer perceives only a tiny fraction of this full reality: she can only see her own Hubble volume (Level I), and decoherence prevents her from perceiving Level III parallel copies of herself. When she is asked a question, makes a snap decision, and answers (Figure 2), quantum effects at the neuron level in her brain lead to multiple outcomes, and from the bird perspective, her single past branches into multiple futures. From their frog perspectives, however, each copy of her is unaware of the other copies, and she perceives this quantum branching as merely a slight sense of randomness: she knows she could have chosen differently, but did not. Afterwards, there are for all practical purposes multiple copies of her that have the exact same memories up until the point when she answers the question.

C. How Many Different Parallel Universes Are There?

Figure 2 illustrates that this exact same situation occurs even in the Level I multiverse, the only difference being where her copies reside. In this sense, Level III is no stranger than Level I. Indeed, if physics is unitary, then the quantum fluctuations during inflation did not generate unique initial conditions through a random process, but rather generated a quantum superposition of all possible initial conditions simultaneously, after which decoherence caused these fluctuations to behave essentially classically in separate quantum branches. The ergodic nature of these quantum fluctuations therefore implies that the distribution of outcomes in a given Hubble volume at Level III (between different quantum branches as in Figure 3) is identical to the distribution that you get by sampling different Hubble volumes within a single quantum branch (Level I). If physical constants can vary as in Level II, then they, too, will vary between parallel quantum branches at Level III. The reason for this is that if physics is unitary, then the process of spontaneous symmetry breaking will not produce a unique (albeit random) outcome, but rather a superposition of all outcomes that rapidly decoheres into separate Level III branches. In short, the Level III multiverse, if it exists, adds nothing new beyond Level I and Level II—just more indistinguishable copies of the same universes, the same old story lines playing out again and again in other quantum branches. The passionate debate about Everett's parallel universes that has raged on for decades therefore seems to be ending in a grand anticlimax, with the discovery of a less controversial multiverse that is just as large.

A common objection is that repeated branching would exponentially increase the number of universes over time. However, the number of universes N may well stay constant. By the number of "universes" N, we mean the number that are indistinguishable from the frog perspective (from the bird perspective, there is of course just one) at a given instant, *i.e.*, the number of macroscopically different Hubble volumes. Although there is obviously a vast number of them with different initial conditions, the number N is clearly finite. The smooth unitary evolution of the wave function in the bird perspective corresponds to a never-ending sliding between these N classical universe snapshots from the frog perspective of an observer. Now you're in universe A, the one where you're reading this sentence. Now you're in universe B, the one where you're reading this other sentence. Put differently, universe B has an observer identical to one in universe A, except with an extra instant of memories. In Figure 2, our observer first finds herself in the universe described by the left panel, but now there are two different universes smoothly connecting to it like B did to A, and in both of these, she will be unaware of the other one. The Level III multiverse thus involves not only splitting branches but merging branches as well.

D. Two Worldviews

The debate over how classical mechanics emerges from quantum mechanics continues, and the decoherence discovery has shown that there is a lot more to it than previously thought. Yet this is just a small piece of a larger puzzle. The endless debate over the interpretation of quantum mechanics—and even the broader issue of parallel universes—is in a sense the tip of an iceberg. In the sci-fi spoof *Hitchhiker's Guide to the Galaxy*, the answer is discovered to be "42," and the hard part is finding the real question. Questions about parallel universes may seem to be just about as deep as queries about reality can get. Yet there is a still deeper underlying question: there are two tenable but diametrically opposed paradigms regarding physical reality and the status of mathematics, a dichotomy that arguably goes as far back as Plato and Aristotle, and the question is—which one is correct?

- **ARISTOTELIAN PARADIGM:** The subjectively perceived frog perspective is physically real, and the bird perspective and all its mathematical language is merely a useful approximation.

- **PLATONIC PARADIGM:** The bird perspective (the mathematical structure) is physically real, and the frog perspective and all the human language we use to describe it is merely a useful approximation for describing our subjective perceptions.

What is more basic—the frog perspective or the bird perspective? What is more basic—human language or mathematical language? Your answer will determine how you feel about parallel universes. If you prefer the Platonic paradigm, you should find multiverses natural, since our feeling that says the Level III multiverse is "weird" merely reflects that the frog and bird perspectives are extremely different. We break the symmetry by calling the latter weird because we were all indoctrinated with the Aristotelian paradigm as children, long before we even heard of mathematics—the Platonic view is an acquired taste!

In the second, Platonic case, all of physics is ultimately a mathematics problem, since an infinitely intelligent mathematician given the fundamental equations of the cosmos could in principle *compute* the frog perspective, *i.e.*, compute what self-aware observers the Universe would contain, what they would perceive, and what language they would invent to describe their perceptions to one another. In other words, there is a "Theory of Everything" (TOE) whose axioms are purely mathematical, since postulates in English regarding interpretation would be derivable, and thus redundant. In the Aristotelian paradigm, on the other hand, there can never be a TOE, since one is ultimately just explaining certain verbal statements by using other verbal statements—this is known as the infinite regress problem (Nozick 1981).

IV. Discussion

We have surveyed scientific theories of parallel universes, and found that they naturally form a hierarchy of multiverses (Figure 1) allowing progressively greater differences from our own Universe:

- **LEVEL I**: Other Hubble volumes have different initial conditions
- **LEVEL II**: Other postinflation bubbles may have different effective laws of physics (constants, dimensionality, particle content)
- **LEVEL III**: Other branches of the quantum wave function add nothing qualitatively new

Whereas the Level I universes join seamlessly, there are clear demarcations between those within Levels II and III caused by inflating space and decoherence, respectively. Few astronomers would suggest that space ends abruptly at the edge of the observable Universe. It is ironic, then, that Level III is the one that has drawn the most fire in the past decades, since it is the only one that adds no qualitatively new types of universes.

A. Future Prospects

There are ample future prospects for testing and perhaps ruling out these multiverse theories. In the coming decade, dramatically improved cosmological measurements of the microwave background radiation, the large-scale matter distribution, etc., will test Level I by further constraining the curvature and topology of space and will test Level II by providing stringent tests of inflation.

Progress in both astrophysics and high-energy physics should also clarify the extent to which various physical constants are fine-tuned, thereby weakening or strengthening the case for Level II. If the current worldwide effort to build quantum computers succeeds, it will provide further evidence for Level III, since they would, in essence, be exploiting the parallelism of the Level III multiverse for parallel computation. Conversely, experimental evidence that contradicts unitary theory would rule out Level III.

B. The Measure Problem

There are also interesting theoretical issues to resolve within the multiverse theories, first and foremost the *measure problem*. As multiverse theories gain credence, the sticky issue of how to compute probabilities in physics is growing from a minor nuisance into a major embarrassment. As noted previously, the reason why probabilities become so important is that if there are indeed many copies of "you" with identical past lives and memories, you could not compute your own future even if you had complete knowledge of the entire state of the multiverse, because there is no way for you to determine which of these copies is "you" (they all feel that they are). All you can predict is therefore probabilities for what you will observe, corresponding to the fractions of these observers that experience different things.

Unfortunately, computing what fraction of the infinitely many observers perceive what is very subtle, since the answer depends on the order in which you count them! The fraction of integers that are even is 50 percent if you order them 1, 2, 3, 4 . . . , but approaches 100 percent if you order them alphabetically the way your word processor would (1, 10, 100, 1000 . . .). When observers reside in disconnected universes, there is no obviously natural way in which to order them, and so to order the different universes, one must use statistical weights, referred to by mathematicians as a "measure." This problem crops up in a mild and treatable manner in Level I, becomes severe at Level II, and has caused much debate within the context of extracting quantum probabilities in Level III.

C. The Pros and Cons of Parallel Universes

So should you believe in parallel universes? Let us conclude with a brief discussion of arguments pro and con. First of all, we have seen that this is not a yes/no question—rather, the most interesting issue is how many levels of multiverses are there? Figure 1 summarizes evidence for the different levels. Cosmology observations support Level I by pointing to a flat infinite space with ergodic matter distribution, and Level I plus inflation elegantly eliminates the initial condition problem. Level II is supported by the success of inflation theory in explaining cosmological observations, and it can explain apparent fine-tuning of physical parameters. Level III is supported by both experimental and theoretical evidence for unitarity, and explains the apparent quantum randomness that bothered Einstein so much without abandoning causality from the bird perspective.

Going from our Universe to the Level I multiverse eliminates the need to specify initial conditions, and upgrading to Level II eliminates the need to specify physical constants. Since it is merely in the frog perspective, in the subjective perceptions of observers, that this opulence of information and complexity is really there, a multiverse theory is arguably more economical than one endowing only a single ensemble element with physical existence.

The argument against multiverse theories is that they are vulnerable to Ockham's razor, since they postulate the existence of other worlds that we can never observe. Principal arguments against parallel universes are that they are wasteful and weird, so let us consider these two objections in turn.

Why should nature be so ontologically wasteful and indulge in such opulence as to contain an infinity of different worlds? Intriguingly, this argument can be turned around to argue *for* a multiverse. When we feel that nature is wasteful, what precisely are we disturbed about her wasting? Certainly not "space," since the standard flat universe model with its infinite volume draws no such objections. Certainly not "mass" or "atoms" either, for the same reason—once you have wasted an infinite amount of something, who cares if you waste some more? Rather, it is probably the apparent reduction in simplicity that appears disturbing, the quantity of information necessary to specify all these unseen worlds. However, an entire ensemble is often much simpler than any one of its members.

The other common complaint about multiverses is that they are weird. This objection is aesthetic rather than scientific, and as mentioned above, really only makes sense in the Aristotelian worldview. In the Platonic paradigm, one might expect observers to complain that the correct Theory of Everything was weird if the bird perspective was sufficiently different from the frog perspective, and there is every indication that this is the case for us. The perceived weirdness is hardly surprising, since evolution provided us with intuition only for the everyday physics that had survival value for our distant ancestors. Thanks to clever inventions, we have glimpsed slightly more than the frog perspective of our normal inside view, and sure enough, we have encountered bizarre phenomena whenever departing from human scales in any way: at high speeds (time slows down), on small scales (quantum particles can be at several places at once), on large scales (black holes), at low temperatures (liquid helium can flow upward), at high temperatures (colliding particles can change identity), etc. As a result, physicists have by and large already accepted that the frog and bird perspectives are very different. Many experimentalists are becoming blasé about producing many "weird" (but perfectly repeatable) experimental results, and simply accept that the world is a weirder place than we thought it was.

We have seen that a common feature of all multiverse levels is that the simplest and most elegant theory involves parallel universes by default, and that adding experimentally unsupported processes and ad hoc postulates to explain away the parallel universes only complicates the theory. Our aesthetic judgement therefore comes down to what we find more wasteful and inelegant: many worlds or many words. Perhaps we will gradually get more used to the weird ways of our cosmos, and even find its strangeness to be part of its charm.

> **MAX TEGMARK, PHD,** is a cosmologist and professor at MIT.

DÉJÀ NEW

Not Quite the Parallel Universe Story We've Seen Before on TV

MIKE BROTHERTON

Working in parallel, astronomer Mike Brotherton, in collaboration with sci-fi novelist Mike Brotherton from Over There, has woven together an essay on the use of the alternate reality as a plot device in works of science fiction over the years, as well as how *Fringe* treats the same topic.

CORRECTION: It has come to our attention that Mike Brotherton, PhD, is both an astronomer and sci-fi novelist. We apologize for any confusion this may have caused.

Parallel universes are popular mainstays in science fiction, but they're more than simply a science-fiction construct. The probabilistic equations of quantum mechanics, and more than a few experiments that spawned them, suggest that parallel universes may be real. One such experiment— usually done only as a thought experiment, thankfully—is the case of Schrödinger's cat.

Put a cat in a box. Add some poison gas with a trigger that depends on a random event: radioactive decay. (According to quantum mechanics, microscopic systems like a radioactive atom exist in a superposition of decayed and undecayed states. It is only when the system interacts with the rest of the world [e.g., an observer] that it is forced to stop this blurry dual existence— called a superposition, or superposed state—and exist as one or the other.) Let some time pass, until there's a 50 percent chance that the poison has been released. Until we check, the cat is *both* alive and dead. A single reality is forced on the cat—the cat only settles on being *either* alive or dead—when someone opens the box to see what is going on inside.

Schrödinger's poor boxed cat, if brought in to Walter's lab to be both autopsied and not autopsied, represents two valid realities, although eventually only one path is taken in our Universe, while a second universe takes the other. As Walter explained in "The Road Not Taken" (1-19) in season one:

> **WALTER:** Most of us experience life as a—a linear progression just like this. [Draws a horizontal line on a

chalkboard.] But this is an illusion because every day, life presents us with an array of choices. As a result, life should look more like this. [Draws diagonal branches from the first line.] And each choice . . . leads to a new path. To go to work. To stay home. And each choice we take creates a new reality. Do—do you understand?

OLIVIA: Yes. But what does it have to do with deja vu?

WALTER: Deja vu is—is—is simply a—a momentary glimpse to the other side.

Almost everyone experiences it. We feel that we've been somewhere before because actually we have—in another reality. It's another path. The road not taken.

In the *Fringe* universe, and perhaps our own as well, every choice splits the Universe. This splitting is not just theoretical. Superposed, blurry states have real existence. There are real-world consequences, as demonstrated by another classic physics experiment: the double slit experiment.

Imagine first shining a light through a narrow slit onto a screen beyond. The screen is most brightly illuminated directly behind the slit, with the intensity dropping off to the sides. Next, replace the single slit with two narrow slits side by side. Something different happens. Light passing through the two slits creates interference patterns on a screen, the same way water waves passing through two side-by-side openings in a reef interact at the shoreline beyond. When two wave crests hit the same location, there is constructive interference: the two crests produce a single higher wave, a brighter light intensity on the screen. When troughs meet, there is destructive interference—a deeper trough, a deep darkness. The two waves interact and combine, creating a complex pattern where bright constructive interference (sometimes called fringes) alternates with dark regions of destruction.

Now, that isn't so weird, perhaps. But it turns out that, according to quantum mechanics, particles like electrons can also act like waves. Classically, we think of an electron as a particle that, when aimed at a screen, can only go through either one slit or the other. But when the experiment is done so that only one electron at a time is sent toward the slits, we still get an interference pattern, the way we do with light and water waves. One interpretation of this result is that the electron goes through *both* slits, representing two distinct realities, and that those two realities interfere with each other.

Humans like to think of a single sequence of events describing history and leading toward our future reality. This is not really the case. The Universe is a lot messier, even though the messy details are not always easily perceived. Microelectronic devices regularly exploit this universal weirdness: the reality of the quantum world that embraces multiple realities simultaneously.

Fringe, among other wonderful things, is a story based on the consequences of quantum mechanics and in particular on one person's path that places two universes into destructive interference. Walter Bishop's love for his son, Peter, leads him to open the door to another universe and threatens the destruction of both, although our realization of this builds slowly an episode at a time. At the start, *Fringe* appears to be a series about FBI agents investigating weird stuff, like *The X-Files*. *Fringe*'s equivalent of *X-Files*' aliens are not aliens, however. They're eventually revealed to be different versions of ourselves. Despite superficial similarities that may initially incite feelings of déjà vu, *Fringe* is not *The X-Files*. *Fringe* is something new.

Alternate Universes on Television

Fringe isn't new in that it's the first television show to take on alternate universes. There's a whole tradition of alternate universes on the small screen.

Arguably the most famous example is the *Star Trek* episode "Mirror Mirror" (2-4), where members of the crew of the *Enterprise* end up in another universe in which everyone seems a little more ruthless, perhaps even a little more evil. Definitely sexier. They gain an ally in that universe's Mr. Spock, whose opposite self is overly ambitious but still pragmatically logical.

(It's a delicious homage that when Olivia Dunham travels to the alternate universe, she meets Spock—I mean, William Bell—played by Leonard Nimoy. It would have been too much to have given him a goatee as in "Mirror Mirror," but the scene is nevertheless rich given the history.)

Later Star Trek series, particularly *Deep Space Nine*, continued using the universe of "Mirror Mirror," showcasing sexier and edgier versions of well-established characters.

One of the best-loved and most entertaining uses of dark, sexy parallel universes comes from Joss Whedon's *Buffy the Vampire Slayer*. Nerdy computer geek Willow's alternate version was a bisexual "Vamp Willow," who sucked blood with the same zest her mousy version hacked passwords, foreshadowing her later development into a powerful and vengeful witch. In addition to the world where vampires took over Sunnydale, there were infinite other universes within the Buffyverse, including an infamous "world without shrimp."

Other TV shows invoking alternate universes include *Charmed*, *Stargate: SG-1*, and *Sliders*, among others. What all these shows have in common is that their use of parallel universes rarely *matters* to the main story line. Alternate universes are single-episode gimmicks, temporary diversions used to highlight character attributes or, as *Buffy*'s world without shrimp to play for laughs. (While the concept of alternate universes was central to *Sliders*, its individual universes were never deeply developed.) *Fringe* is special because the alternate universe concept is fundamental to the show, something that spawns a unique type of story.

Fringe owes its ability to tell the story it does to a recent change in television storytelling and series like *Buffy*, *Babylon 5*, and *Lost*, which established the seasonal or multiseasonal story. This is an innovation that may be as important as the novel. Back in the 1960s when mirror Spock sported a goatee, stories lasted an episode and at the end everything was restored to the series default so the next set of writers could launch their tale. Miniseries, a format developed in the late 1970s, let creators tell longer stories, but it was the 1990s before fifteen to twenty or more hours became a viable storytelling length. In this sense, *Fringe* is a twenty-first-century show, with story arcs that build episode to episode, even season to season.

Story arcs that span seasons also allow something new that has rarely been seen in television or movies: alternate world-building, the process of creating a fictional reality. And this is what allows *Fringe* to take on alternate universes with a depth and thoroughness that no other television show has yet achieved.

Fringe and Alternate Universes

Fringe wasn't up front about its deep storytelling, but the seeds were there in the early episodes, slowly revealed: a striptease if you will. (Is it a coincidence that strippers have appeared in several episodes?) *Fringe* started on the fringe, with what looked like a world much as our own, a drama pitting the FBI against bioterrorists, only slowly trickling in the weird stuff. Except for Walter Bishop—he was wonderfully weird from the start, and appropriately so given that his history is what drives the entire series.

This is stealth science fiction, much like *Lost*. It looks like our world, feels like our world, with interesting characters grappling with something strange, but only a little strange. Looks can be deceiving.

While a lot of early episodes could be characterized as "monster of the week" tales, they're establishing character and more. They lay important groundwork, deliberately sucking in a general audience and converting them into believers in fringe phenomena the way Agent Mulder and the evidence brought the rational, logical Scully to the crazy but evidence-based perspective of *The X-Files* reality.

Episodes that on the surface have little to do with the overarching plotline of the war between alternate Earths actually slip in details that establish the premise in subtle ways, quite satisfying in hindsight. For instance, in the first-season episode "Inner Child" (1-15) Peter gave a boy (apparently a young observer) a GI Joe action figure. His line was the following:

PETER: It's funny, I remember the scar being on the other side . . .

Since Walter's memory is shot, it seems natural that Walter and Peter don't remember the same things. It is anything but natural. They have memories of being together, but they weren't. The toys of Peter's youth were not the toys he actually played with.

Incidents like these are hints to Peter's nature and upbringing being stranger than anyone realizes. The creators of *Fringe* know where they're going, and they're going deep right from the start. They're planning to suck everyone along into their alternate reality, and their slow, subtle plan succeeds.

At first we only get glimpses into the alternate universe, shimmering windows in space, Olivia's extended déjà vu, before we visit for longer periods. Its striptease is a skilled one, making us excited and wanting to see more. *Fringe* is no nervous schoolgirl; *Fringe* is a sophisticated seductress, and viewers can't look away. Each glimpse begets a dozen questions, and each of those question leads to more questions, in a pattern that Walter could draw on a blackboard and use to explain how universes split: we could pursue the answer to *this* question, or *that* one, or another one altogether.

To realize the power of this seduction, imagine a description of one of the early episodes, for example the pilot: "FBI agents try to figure out who is responsible for the release of a deadly biological agent on an international flight." Then imagine the summary of a second-season episode, "Momentum Deferred" (2-4), and how it might read: "Agent Dunham races a mercury-blooded shape-shifting soldier from another universe to secure the frozen head of a person of interest." Not exactly a story line as easily absorbed as the pilot, is it? But by the second season, *Fringe* has its audience assimilated, so to speak, into the wacky world of quantum mechanics and Walter Bishop. By the third season, episodes occur entirely within the world of the alternate universe. It's normal. For *Fringe*.

By this third season, *Fringe* is well into its alternate world-building. The alternate universe is a place where everyone is almost the same but more evil. Or sexier (depending how you feel about Olivia as a smirking redhead). Or a vampire. That other world and the people who live there are similar enough to be easily recognizable, although significant differences exist.

The alternate Earth is still our Earth, but different in ways our own world could have been different. Our first clear look at the other world: the twin towers of the World Trade Center standing tall and straight in the sunlight. Visually and emotionally *stunning*.

But wait, there's more. The American flag has forty-eight stars instead of fifty. Twenty-dollar bills sport Martin Luther King Jr. and are in fact called "Juniors." John F. Kennedy was never assassinated and became ambassador to the United Nations, while Richard Nixon ended up on silver dollars.

The map of the United States seen in the Secretary of Defense's office differs fundamentally from our own in a number of ways, both obvious and subtle. Some dual states have been combined, like Dakota and Carolina. So have some less obvious dual states, like Oklahoma and Kansas, which have merged into the state of Midland. Texas is split into North Texas and South Texas. Some states are not even states, like Nevada, which is Independent Nevada, and Louisiana is a territory. Michigan has lost its northern peninsula. California has lost its coast. We're not in Kansas anymore. That's part of *Midland* now, remember?

The people in the other world are more technologically advanced in many ways. They had cell phones and CD players in their cars in the mid-1980s. Their medicine is better and faster, employing nanotechnology. Dirigibles float in city skies.

The creators of *Fringe* have not limited themselves to differences in technology and government. Culture and entertainment vary as well. *The West Wing* has run for eleven seasons and airs in a 5 P.M. Sunday time slot. Eric Stolz got the lead in *Back to the Future* rather than Michael J. Fox. *Dogs* plays on Broadway rather than *Cats*.

Perhaps some of these changes are just for fun and shock value, but there are a lot of them and they represent a real effort at world-building.

The people in the two universes often look alike, and act alike, but can be profoundly different. Married in one reality, single in the other. Or, like Peter, dead in one reality and alive in the other. Olivia and Walter have their doubles, Fauxlivia and Walternate. The two Olivias have a lot of similarities but surface differences. The Walters are a whole different story.

Walternate, because of the loss of his son, won't experiment on children. Walter has never seemed to have a problem experimenting on anything, although something prevented him from developing into the more ruthless man he was becoming. Maybe his voluntary brain surgery. Or perhaps the years in the mental institution. Anyway, the Walters are both brilliant, but their histories have left them at odds.

When Walter stole Walternate's son, he launched the pattern of destructive interference and the resulting war between worlds. Which reminds us that the crisis is not the result of random events like radioactive decay, but rather the actions of people (who think about putting cats in dangerous boxes and will take huge risks for their own emotional well-being). Fundamentally, people matter in *Fringe*. The entire unraveling of reality, the vortexes, the destruction, all result from Walter's obsessive love of family. In the third-season episode "6B" (3-14), the concept of "emotional quantum entanglement" is introduced to explain how and why people can bridge the universes. (Quantum entanglement was also the explanation given at the end of season three for why Walternate activating the doomsday machine in his universe also activated the machine in ours: because the two are quantum entangled, what happens to one affects what happens to the other.) Quantum entanglement describes the existence of a relationship between what comes out of those blurry, interfering, superposed light waves, electrons, and cats. A pattern. In *Fringe*, science and human desire are intertwined, lending an emotional component to the equations. Human relationships and their different forking paths interfere with themselves, interacting across the universes, possibly leading to destruction. A coin flip, a random event like the radioactive decay that threatens the life of Schrödinger's cat, creates linked outcomes: one spouse dies while the other lives, but with opposite outcomes in the two universes. Their relationship, their urge to stay connected, threatens annihilation. In this way, the individual episode "6B" echoes the entire story arc of *Fringe*.

The alternate universe is not just an interesting place to see Walter, Olivia, and our own world in a fun-house mirror. *Fringe* is a story about the reality of quantum mechanics, what the multiple universes imply, and how those universes can interfere with each other, a more sophisticated idea than we usually find in science-fiction and fantasy television. There's substance here.

But though that level of substance may have only now reached television, it has long been present in literature.

Fringe's Literary Forebears

Fringe is deeply steeped in the literary sci-fi tradition and often pays homage to its inspirations.[1] In the season-two episode "Jacksonville" (2-15) there is a building that, shall we say, interferes with itself across the two universes. Destructively. This is the Zelazny building. Roger Zelazny was a science-fiction writer who penned the classic novel *Nine Princes in Amber*, about an exile who loses his memory and is trapped in a foreign universe. It is likely not a coincidence that in the alternate universe they use a substance called "amber" to plug the holes between the realities. But it is the way *Fringe* uses the science behind parallel universes to enrich its story that most thoroughly recalls the literary science-fiction tradition—including comics.

In particular, the sci-fi subgenre of alternate history uses the idea of parallel universes as the basis for in-depth world-building. Alternate history is a variation of science fiction in which the story is set in a parallel universe in which some key event has transpired differently, as in the Hugo award–winning novel *The Man in the High Castle* by Philip K. Dick. Dick's story takes place in an America that lost World War II to the Axis

---

1   Editor's note: see also Paul Levinson's and Amy H. Sturgis' essays.

forces. While that might be viewed as a dystopia, other alternate histories are utopias, like L. Neil Smith's 1980 novel, *The Probability Broach*, a Libertarian fantasy in which George Washington was killed during the Whiskey Rebellion and the Constitution was never the law of the land. There are a host of others.

One of the most famous examples is Jorge Luis Borges' 1941 short story "The Garden of Forking Paths," a classic used in English classes, about a world in which all possible choices are considered simultaneously, eliminating all but one as we do when we live in a single universe. Walter's chalkboard scribbles when he explained déjà vu to Olivia in "The Road Not Taken" illustrated forking paths.

Comic books (just a different side of the literary coin) have also featured more in-depth parallel universes. Marvel Comics has had several runs of a series called "What if . . . " that used the concept of forking paths. The first issue asked, "What if Spider-Man had joined the Fantastic Four?" Spider-Man approached them in his own first issue back in 1963, under the impression they had nice salaries and benefits. Apparently they weren't even at FBI levels and it didn't work out. (Interestingly, the "What if . . . " series was narrated by an alien character called "The Watcher," a bald man of great power who did not interfere in the Marvel universe and who has a strong resemblance to the Observers in *Fringe*.) Later, Marvel Comics killed off *Fantastic Four* member the Human Torch, and his replacement was none other than Spider-Man.

More so than even Marvel, DC Comics really went with the concept of the multiverse. In order to reconcile the existence of both World War II and modern versions of their superheroes like Superman and Green Lantern, as well as properties purchased from other comic book companies such as Captain

Marvel and the entire Marvel family, DC used parallel universes. Modern superheroes existed on Earth 1, World War II era on Earth 2, etc. DC also published a series of comics detailing a story line called "Crisis on Infinite Earths" in which these universes were merging, destructively.

It doesn't seem that the creators of *Fringe* are ignorant of these stories, as DC Comics covers were featured in the second part of the season-two finale, "Over There" (2-23). In *Fringe*'s Earth 2, Green Lantern and Green Arrow had traded their colors for the more dangerous red, a likely homage to the DC crisis.

The homages are enjoyable Easter eggs for fans of literary science fiction and comics to discover, but they also acknowledge *Fringe*'s debt to these earlier parallel universe stories. The small screen too often reinvents the wheel, and doesn't do it as well. *Fringe* is a welcome exception that acknowledges its influences and builds on them in a new format.

Peeking Behind the Curtain of *Fringe*

The *Fringe* that we've watched develop over the past few seasons is as distinct from a paranormal FBI show like *The X-Files* as it is from a parallel universe show like *Sliders* that never developed its worlds. Consider the man behind the curtain in *The Wizard of Oz* (another tale of travel to an alternate reality, not Kansas or even Midland). The wizard was just a man with some tricks, not the fearsome figure he made himself appear to be. To keep the sense of power and magic, people were advised to "pay no attention to the man behind the curtain!"

That seems to have been part of the formula of shows like *The X-Files*: give the audience glimpses, but never the full monty. Explaining the mysteries might spoil the effect and leave viewers ultimately disappointed.

Fringe has a different formula, perhaps more powerful. The curtain continuously moves back to expose its secrets. The secrets are satisfying, and it is not a man revealed, but an entire world. *The X-Files* was unable to deliver that in the end. *Fringe* has gone to a place *The X-Files* never did, and beyond, while paying homage to its inspirations. It isn't yet clear whether or not *Fringe's* alternate Earth has shrimp, however (although avocados are apparently hard to come by).

As an Observer once noted in an episode of the same name, "There is more than one of everything" ("There's More Than One of Everything," 1-20). There have been a number of television shows involving FBI investigators, strange phenomena, and parallel universes. Nevertheless, it's not quite déjà vu with *Fringe*. The program is a welcome pioneer for television, invoking a literary tradition and making the science matter.

And speaking of that science . . . one has to suspect that the alternate universe's Schrödinger has a thought experiment involving a dog rather than a cat. *Fringe* may be deep, but it's also always fun.

⋎ MIKE BROTHERTON is the author of the science-fiction novels *Star Dragon* (2003) and *Spider Star* (2008), both from Tor Books. He's also a professor of astronomy at the University of Wyoming and conducts research on active galaxies using the Hubble Space Telescope and nearly every observatory that will give him time in their facilities. He is the founder of the NASA-and National Science Foundation-funded Launch Pad Astronomy Workshop for Writers, which brings a dozen award-winning professional writers to Wyoming every summer. He blogs about science and science fiction at www.mikebrotherton.com and tries to keep his cat, Sita, out of boxes.

THE MALLEABILITY OF MEMORY

GARTH SUNDEM

Human memory: impermanent, fallible, malleable. Garth Sundem discusses how, on *Fringe*, Peter Bishop's dearth of memories can be seen as ... as ... what was I saying again?

While *Fringe* is shot through with the paranormal, its bread and butter is the leading edge of the very *normal* science of memory—how do we make it, store it, and retrieve it? Walter can't remember much of anything, Olivia can't remember her childhood but remembers everything else, and Peter forgets little things like the fact he came from a different universe. And pushing memories around like pucks on a shuffleboard strip drives many of the show's weekly plots—characters attempt to regain memories, steal them, repress them, and replace them, usually in rather suspenseful, medically explicit, and action-packed ways. While the specifics of these ways step slightly over the line from science to fiction, the show's theoretical take on what's possible in the weird and wild world of memory is spot on.

Throughout the seasons and episodes of *Fringe*, it's as if creators and writers Abrams, Kurtzman, Orci, and company read psychology journals over their morning coffee and then wondered *what if...*? What if memory B cells held experiences other than pathogens? What if memories could be *physically* removed from one mind and inserted into others? What if mind-expansion drugs could make someone eidetic or psychic? Really, that's how the best sci-fi gets born: What if mosquitoes encased in amber held dinosaur DNA (*Jurassic Park*)? What if you'd stepped on a prehistoric butterfly ("A Sound of Thunder")? What would life look like on a planet almost completely devoid of water (*Dune*) or a planet completely covered by water (*Waterworld* ... okay, that one sucked, but you get the point)?

So if *Fringe*'s what-ifs sprout from the truth like somewhat fanciful flowers, the first step in distinguishing memory fact from memory fiction is to dig through the soil: what is memory? What are its limits and loopholes?

It's nice to imagine memory as a slightly fuzzier version of Olivia's ability to instantly imprint things like the ID number on a cabbie's Show Me card—that our memories are the lingering impressions of things that actually happened, and that while a memory might omit details, everything that's included was at one time real. It happened. And our brain simply grabs whatever it can of these experiences and files memories in discreet little drawers somewhere in the folds of our grey matter until they're needed at some later date.

It's a nice theory, but as we see in *Fringe* (and in real life), it's completely, patently, bodaciously wrong.

Memory is malleable. How you get it, how you store it, and how you retrieve it can all be punk'd, sometimes in ways eerily similar to techniques in *Fringe* that you hoped were fanciful, and sometimes in ways so simple that you could do it tomorrow with your unsuspecting work buddies.

First, let's break it down old school and look at how memories are formed.

Your senses collect new experiences and filter them toward the hippocampus, which is a nifty little processing center that accepts the delivery of experiences and bundles them for storage. It's very easy: experiences come in, and the hippocampus packages them and spits them back out—end of story. Nearly all of our memories are created this way.

But science is just now exploring a potential work-around, as seen in the case of British musician Clive Wearing. In 1985,

Wearing contracted a virus that ate his hippocampus (very much like the flesh-dissolving agent that munched Olivia's honey in season one). Gone. Nixed. Nada. Completely pruned from the brain. And thus pruned, Wearing completely lost the ability to code new memories. Interestingly, largely unimpaired were his working memory (allowing him to manipulate the stored information needed to read and socialize), his short-term memory (allowing him to retain facts for short periods of time), and his long-term memory (allowing him to recall events prior to his surgery). He continued to perform normally on IQ tests. Only, Wearing stayed trapped in 1985, where he went second-by-second about his day but where things inexplicably changed minute-by-minute—a door was open instead of closed; his wife, Deborah, was there, and then gone; things popped into and out of existence. But, almost cruelly, Wearing retained the ability to grow bits of *implicit* memory—somewhere in his unconscious he was able to hold and retain the impression that something was very wrong with him. And while he couldn't consciously remember the names of prime ministers, he might blurt out, "John Major Vehicle!" when looking at a car with license plate JMV (Major was prime minister in the 1990s).

There may soon be hope for patients like Wearing and others unable to code new memories. Because the hippocampus is so much like an old-school telephone routing board—a little spitting of electricity in, and a corresponding little spitting of electricity out—researchers at USC were able to program these ins and outs onto a computer chip, creating an artificial hippocampus, capable of taking the place of a damaged hippocampus as surely as a hook replaces a hand. This neuroprosthetic is making its way toward humans.

Does this sound familiar? It should. It was what Newton did to Walter in the episode "Grey Matters" (2-10). Long ago, William Bell removed three pieces of Walter's hippocampus (the science of which is on shaky footing, see below)—ones that stored the memory of how to open the door to the other side. Later, Newton reclaimed these pieces (surgically!) from their hosts and tried to plug them back into Walter's brain, which was the only tool that could interpret them. That was, if they were reconnected correctly. Newton hooked Walter to a machine and showed Walter pictures of memories—most powerfully a coffin that we assume held the young, real-world Peter—and as Walter pulled these memories through the mechanics of his brain, the machine mapped the pathways this information took. What inputs led to what outputs in Walter's hippocampus? If Newton could determine how memories are routed, he could then align the removed tissue in a way that allowed it to reconnect to Walter's brain. (This is a perfect example of *Fringe* being conceptually spot on, but a bit fiction-y in the specifics: to map Walter's hippocampus they should've had him code *new* memories, rather than recall old ones—but that would've nixed a valuable opportunity to fill in tasty tidbits of Walter's backstory.)

So senses collect, the hippocampus processes, and then memories are offloaded to dusty storage closets distributed throughout the brain. (Thus, as above, the description in "Grey Matters" of Paris removing these three sections of memory from Walter's *hippocampus* was a bit off.) And once memories are bundled and stored, the hippocampus is off the hook. You could grind it into hippo-paté and it wouldn't affect the tiny bundles of long-term memory that have already passed safely through. This is why Clive Wearing, with his hippocampus dissolved, kept his long-term memories but lost the ability to code new ones.

But notice that nowhere in this process of memory acquisition is the information hitting the hippocampus required to be *real* experiences—this allows us to learn word-of-mouth from others' experiences as well as our own. Still, this is a long way from some of the memory tricks we see in *Fringe*. Is it conceivable to surgically implant Walter's memories into the three extras who donated fourteen years of their lives to carrying Walter's recollections of how to open a door?

Surgically, no. But why would you use a knife when it's so very, very easy to create false memories without all that messy slicing and dicing?

The go-to researcher on false memories is Elizabeth Loftus, who's been wiring foreign material into subjects' memory webs since the 1970s. In the first of a series of famous experiments, Loftus had parents implant into their children the false memory of being lost in a shopping mall. The parent started with something like, "Remember the time you were lost in the mall?" And at first, the kids tended to deny the false memory—no, of course they had no recollection of this thing that never happened. But as parents provided more false details—"Don't you remember, we agreed to meet at the tug boat?"—kids started to "remember" on their own, adding their own details to this false memory.

This experiment elicited a deluge of skepticism. Couldn't it be possible that, rather than actually adopting a false memory, kids were simply being agreeable, playing along with a parent who so obviously *wanted* them to remember being lost in the mall (for whatever unfathomable parental reason)?

To counter the skeptics, Loftus designed a new study with a couple of rather nifty tweaks on the procedure. First, she used a questionnaire to gather all sorts of information about college-aged subjects' pasts, specifically about foods they liked and disliked. Then she told subjects that the research team had fed their information into a supercomputer that knew, based on this information, what happened to the subjects as children. The "computer" presented subjects with a list that included many of the subjects' real experiences, and within these was intermixed one false experience—in the case of these studies, suggesting the false memory of getting sick from dill pickles, hardboiled eggs, or another food.

And then Loftus served them lunch.

Without prompting, subjects generally avoided the foods that supposedly made them sick as kids but ate as normal everything else on the plate. In other words, they weren't simply paying lip service to a memory they didn't really have in order to please parents or scientists, but somehow this false memory of child-hood food illness had infiltrated their consciousness to the point that it affected their present actions.

It's as if a story told as truth can trick the hippocampus into bundling it in the same way the organ would bundle a real experience.

But in terms of false memory, the hippocampus is just the start. It works in a kind of Laurel and Hardy duo with the amyg-dala, with the hippocampus being the straight man who pretty much repeats what it (thinks it) sees and the amygdala providing the color. After the hippocampus straps a memory into a nice little bundle, the amygdala gets to attach an emotional tag—and these tags are hugely subjective, based not on events themselves but on how you interpret them.

These emotional keywords have obvious evolutionary purpose: fear makes you wary. Remember the last time you nearly fell off a cliff, or crashed your car, or petted a cobra? That wasn't such a good idea, was it? You now know to avoid these things because of the amygdala's pairing of memory with negative emotion.

Was the roller-coaster ride exciting, or scary? Was the dip in the pool cold, or invigorating? Then when we encounter a similar situation—another roller coaster, or another pool—we run a quick keyword search of our memory and check the emotional tag to help us respond to and interpret the new event. Whether you go on the roller coaster or jump in the pool depends on how you tagged these experiences last time.

This gets more interesting when you consider that we all might use different keywords to tag the same event. These keyword tags become part of our reality, and thus perhaps on a more metaphorical scale than *Fringe* we create differing "realities," affecting not just our feelings but our actual recollections of the facts of events themselves.

Elizabeth Loftus (and John Palmer) showed this by forcing their own keyword tags onto subjects' memories. They had subjects watch a video of a car crash and then asked them to estimate the cars' speeds. But the sneaky experimenters phrased the question five slightly different ways:

1. About how fast were the cars going when they hit each other?
2. About how fast were the cars going when they smashed each other?

3. About how fast were the cars going when they collided with each other?

4. About how fast were the cars going when they bumped into each other?

5. About how fast were the cars going when they contacted with each other?

And so they tagged subjects' memories with the keywords *hit, smashed, collided, bumped,* and *contacted.* Subjects' speed estimates when tagged with "smash" averaged nine miles per hour faster than their estimates when tagged with "contact."

Even spookier, though, is that this tagging didn't just affect peoples' speed estimates; it seemed to change their *memories* of the event itself. A week later when Loftus and Palmer asked subjects if the crash had produced broken glass, those whose memories were tagged with "smashed" said yes, while those whose memories had been tagged with "contacted" said no. For, of course, a *smash* breaks glass while a *contact* doesn't.

So specific memories—maybe of a girl in a red dress or a preoccupation with the number twenty-eight—can be inserted in two ways: a false memory via the hippocampus or a false interpretation via the amygdala.

And now we have something safely stored. Whatever it is—real or fake, explicit or implicit, tagged with positive or negative emotion—the trick becomes holding on to it.

According to UCLA memory specialist Robert Bjork, we don't forget anything—we all have Olivia's eidetic memory. His work shows that whatever we experience, we process and store. You say you can't remember your childhood best friend's telephone number? Bjork has shown that if you're reminded of this number, you'll learn it much more quickly and accurately than if you were learning a fresh ten-digit number, meaning that while it may be difficult to retrieve, the memory lives in there somewhere.

So why, then, if all experiences are stored and never fully forgotten, can't you remember where you put your damn car keys in the morning? Bjork calls this a problem not of storage but of retrieval. Is the solution to the problem of the missing keys as simple as Newton's method of slicing open the back of your head with a surgical laser, removing the pulsing chunk of brain that holds this memory, and setting it next to your coffee cup on the kitchen table?

Not so much.

The biggest problem with surgical retrieval is that after the hippocampus, memory doesn't stay bundled—instead of a discreet little package filed in a brain drawer that could be surgically opened and pilfered, one memory seems formed from a little bit of this and a little bit of that, stored willy-nilly throughout the brain.

And so the process of recalling a memory is like rolling a snowball—a trigger like the smell of cotton candy, or the sound of circus music, or the sight of a fun-house mirror provides the first ball, which then rolls through various parts of your brain picking up the additional elements it needs to form the full memory of the time you visited the state fair as a young child. How can you prune a memory if it doesn't live in one, pruneable place?

But while this means that surgical removal of memories is likely to stay fiction, *drugging* away the ability to retrieve a memory is quickly becoming science.

When a trigger hits your brain, a molecule called PKMzeta chooses the paths this little snowball takes, allowing the nascent memory to gather all the relevant bits of info. The more frequently you remember something, the more you reinforce these PKMzeta pathways, making the memory easier to access next time. Without PKMzeta, you can roll a memory snowball and it won't pick up anything.

Now imagine being able to block this PKMzeta exactly when you want. This is what the chemical ZIP does. After teaching rats that certain places in the floor of their cage held electric shocks, researchers injected the rats' brains with ZIP and rats "forgot" their training—in fact, this *forgetting* was blocked recall, as ZIP impeded PKMzeta from doing its snowball work. Another injection of ZIP blocked rats' recall of a sour taste (perhaps another injection would help the rats forget why they're pissed off at the researchers). Soon when you sit down on a barstool, ZIP or chemicals like it could stop the memory of smoking— helping you forget to light up. Or it could (potentially) be made to stop the retrieval of certain memories, for example a soldier's memory of battle trauma.

On the side of aiding rather than blocking retrieval, it's unlikely that we'll be able to biologically "re-grow" memories, like Walter in "Reciprocity" (3-11), anytime soon. But Walter and Olivia both depend on another strategy that you could use tomorrow morning to help you find your keys: Olivia's visit to Jacksonville could help her remember how to cross between worlds, or Walter could jump-start his memory with music, foods, etc.

Triggers as memory aides are firmly within the realm of fact. Remember how a memory starts: a trigger rolls the first small snowball through the brain—they "spark" your memory. And these triggers needn't be explicit—rather than re-creating your walk in the door after work last night, the simple sound of a bell could remind you of your keys' jingle as they landed on the back of the couch (bingo!). These subliminal triggers are so strong that researchers have shown that watching someone sneeze can make you overestimate your chance of dying in a car crash—the sneeze is a trigger that tumbles through your mind and brings to the forefront the idea of your mortality. Or holding a warm drink makes you like people more than if you were holding a cold drink—this warmth triggers feelings and memories of comfort and other general goodness, which you then apply to your companion. Or seeing the color orange during the Halloween season triggers purchasing unrelated orange products. Similarly, the place you learned something becomes bundled with the memory—if you study in a dorm room, you would do best if tested in the same dorm room. And if you learned how to cross from one world to the next in Jacksonville, you're most likely to remember it in the same place.

But we still haven't answered our earlier question: With unlimited storage and triggered recall, why can't we recall every-thing? Why don't we all have Olivia's eidetic memory? Let's check in one final time with Dr. Bjork, who says that our understanding of memory and forgetting as sworn enemies is misleading. Can you remember your zip code? Sure you can. But imagine if you held equally in your brain all the zip codes of all the places you've ever lived. When you're asked to provide the current code, you'd have to sift through all the possibilities before returning the one you want. Instead, our brain prioritizes memories—and the most distant ones, those with the least priority, we count as so meaningless and irrelevant to our current and future choices that we allow them to become inaccessible. At least for now.

Did Olivia really *forget* her childhood spent as a test subject for Walter and William Bell? No. It's there—it's just buried. Did she really forget herself when she was overwritten with the memories of Fauxlivia? Hmmm, now *there's* an interesting question.

Does it seem as if nearly every *Fringe* episode is enriched by a close-up of a syringe puncturing human flesh? And does any episode use the technique to more disturbing effect than "Olivia" (3-1), in which our good heroine became a human pincushion to Walternate and his minions? In that episode, Olivia had to fend off not only the drugs designed to overwrite her, but the attempts of an otherworld psychologist to convince Olivia that the self she brought into the room was not her true self. This was brainwashing, and its portrayal in *Fringe* mirrors its use by cults, governments, and armies through history.

First, let's take a look at the drugs.

It's a nifty idea to inject Olivia with B-lymphocytes, because these cells do, in fact, have a sort of rudimentary memory. B-lymphocytes are the immune system enforcers that both emit antibodies in the presence of a pathogen and then remember these pathogens' signature, allowing them to quickly emit these same antibodies if the pathogen ever shows up again. They're why you only get chicken pox once, or why today you don't get chicken pox at all—after seeing killed virus in a vaccine, B-lymphocytes become what are called "memory B" cells. Thus forever transformed, they're primed for the kill, carrying the memory of the pathogen. What if more than pathogens created memory B cells? What if memory B cells carried actual memories? Then, theoretically, if you removed these memory B cells from one person and injected them into another—with the help of mystery white and blue fluids—you just might transfer memories, mightn't you?

But even without the drugs, the combination of confinement and psychological attack to which Olivia was subjected can do the brainwashing trick just fine.

Central to the definition of brainwashing is its ability to adjust not only your beliefs, but your values. It's not simply that Olivia was meant to believe that she won an Olympic medal for sharp shooting, but that she should adopt the agenda and morality of the otherworld government—just as Patty Hearst was brainwashed into adopting the agenda of her bank-robbing kidnappers, or captured American soldiers during the Korean War were brainwashed into adopting the beliefs of the communist, totalitarian country.

No matter the goals of brainwashing, there are a couple of common steps. First, the victim can't be allowed to meet her own needs, instead depending on her captors or controllers for food, water, information, etc. With self-reliance thus removed, captors can more easily go about the business of stripping away the victim's psychological self by systematically denying everything the victim believes to be true—that Olivia is from another world, that she has no tattoos, etc. Eventually nothing should remain of the victim's self but the intense notion that the self is bad. At this point, brainwashers offer an alternative: communism, cultism, Fauxlivia. And this system offers salvation, as if saying, "Look, it's not you that's bad, it's your mistaken beliefs." And choosing to adopt the new beliefs allows the victim to rebuild a new, very different self, one the victim now believes to be so much better than the old self.

(Likewise, Walter and his wife overwrote Peter. In the episode "Subject 13" [3-15], we saw Peter as a child, recently kidnapped from the other world. As vehemently as Peter insisted that Walter and his wife were not his real parents, Walter insisted that Peter was sick for a long time and simply remembered it wrong. Finally, and especially with young Olivia as a kind of bait for belief in this real world, Peter accepted the brainwashing. By the time of the show's pilot, Peter had entirely forgotten his other-world origins; he had been completely overwritten.)

But even aided by the three-part cocktail of memory-replacement drugs—"another dose of which may kill her!"—Olivia resisted this brainwashing. How did she do it? Let's look again at the Korean War, which provided a large enough brain-washing data set to discover some of the factors that make people more or less susceptible to being overwritten. It turns out that the most distinct factor that predicts successful brainwashing is how concretely you believe things before brainwashing starts. But it's the flip of what you might think—interestingly, American soldiers who originally held rigid belief systems were more likely to flip and adopt communism, while soldiers whose original beliefs were flexible were more likely to bend their beliefs while in captivity and spring back to their original values once released.

And Olivia, who is every day forced to admit the existence of grey area between possible and impossible, would necessarily have flexible beliefs. She can bend without breaking, holding onto her original self even in the face of facts that seem to contradict it.

In fact, this bending encapsulates *Fringe*'s take on memory science as a whole. They flex but don't break it, stretching science like saltwater taffy but stopping just short of the snapping point. In the immortal words of the great TV philosopher Homer Simpson, "It's funny because it's true," and in the case of *Fringe*, it's frightening and fascinating and forceful specifically because it's all possible—or at least plausible—firmly planted in that very sweet spot between science and fiction. *Fringe* hangs its hat on fact: memory is weird and wild, and at the end of the day, nearly as *malleable* as *Fringe* would have us believe.

> ☉ **GARTH SUNDEM** is the author of *Brain Candy*, *The Geeks' Guide to World Domination*, and *Brain Trust: 85 Top Scientists Reveal Lab-Tested Secrets to Surfing, Dating, Dieting, Gambling, Growing Man-Eating Plants and More*. He blogs at Wired's GeekDad, *Psychology Today*, and Science20.com and is a frequent speaker in places where geeks gather. Follow him @garthsundem or find him at garthsundem.com. He recently moved to Boulder, CO, with his psychologist wife and two young kids, the latter of which he hopes will not remember their abduction from the other world.

FRINGE DISEASES

JOVANA GRBIĆ

The *Fringe* culture grows on you. Few viewers exposed to its first-season episodes found the show particularly infectious; in fact many viewers cast a jaundiced eye toward the Fringe Division as bad Mulder and Scully clones. By season two, *Fringe* seemed to chart a new vector and find its direction. It saw an outbreak of new viewers: its popularity went viral and viewership grew at a fevered pitch. This growth in popularity reflects the more literal infections germane to *Fringe*, whose role Jovana Grbić, PhD, clarifies.

Fringe is not a show about biology or infectious diseases in the same way that *Breaking Bad* inherently incorporates chemistry or *CSI* is naturally about forensics. Of the three-plus seasons to date, only a handful of episodes directly deal with communicable diseases, bioweapons, and the threat posed therein.

In fact, the season-two episode "What Lies Below" (2-13) is probably the only stand-alone episode of the series to date centered around a traditional infectious disease plot. In the opening, a man walked into a modern corporate penthouse for a meeting only to collapse, with his veins erupting and spraying blood everywhere. Shortly thereafter, the man who attended to him died from the same symptoms, leading Walter Bishop, the Fringe FBI team, and the lightning-quick on-the-scene CDC to declare a quarantine due to a contagion. A two-block radius was sealed with a barrier, and the office workers were segregated into groups—those who were near the victim and those who weren't—for the purpose of determining whether the virus was airborne. Walter took samples, and ultimately the virus was revealed to have been unearthed from miles below the surface of the Earth by a shady oil company, and was supposedly responsible for wiping out the majority of life during the Ice Age. In the cleverest twist of the episode, Walter postulated that the sulfur in volcanic ash killed off the ancient virus when a volcano erupted back then, and concocted a cure with some horseradish from the refrigerator.

This episode of *Fringe* got some things very right. The quarantine was performed perfectly (though, small gripe: if the virus was airborne, most modern ventilation systems would expose everyone in the building regardless of whether they were near the victim). Walter's cure, horseradish, is in fact very high in sulfur content and has been shown in laboratory tests to be an effective antibiotic. The CDC team's solution, spraying the building with aerosolized sulfur-based neuraminidase blockers, was even plausible. Neuraminidases are enzymes that can cleave a virus from the surface of a newly infected host cell, which makes such enzymes attractive drug targets; drugs such as Tamiflu are neuraminidase inhibitors.

But it also got a lot wrong. In reality, the CDC has very little oversight anywhere in the US states or internationally. They are often not even the first response on the scene for an incident like the one in this episode. The only exception to this is during a national emergency, which would come via a presidential declaration. (Perhaps this is what happened in the episode?) In addition, Walter walked into the isolated makeshift Biosafety Level 4 lab without a sealed suit and was allowed to take samples of a potentially airborne virus back to his own lab for experimentation in open air. Under no conditions would this ever be allowed to happen. He also concocted an almost instantaneous DNA-based test for viral presence based on a cheek swab from a sample of the virus located on the premises. The virus seemed to kill its victims in thirty minutes to two hours, so viral loads would presumably skyrocket exponentially, but cheek swab DNA tests for viruses are only now beginning to be developed for established viruses such as HIV. Lastly, the CDC expert declared this a "Level 6" emergency, which does not exist, necessitating the so-called nuclear option of killing everyone inside. On a recent visit to the CDC, I asked the director of the

Epidemic Intelligence Service if a scenario like this (famously portrayed in the film *Outbreak*) would ever occur. He assured me that this was purely fiction.

The idea that this virus killed off the majority of life during the Ice Age was also somewhat far-fetched. Yes, an unchecked viral or bacterial infection could do a lot of damage. Of the five deadliest pandemics ever recorded,[1] the Plague of Justinian in A.D. 541 killed approximately a quarter of the human population in the Eastern Mediterranean, the Black Death in the fourteenth century killed about 25 percent of the European population, and the deadliest of them all—the Spanish Flu of 1918—killed between 20 and 100 million people worldwide. That's a lot of people, but none of these came close to wiping out the entirety of a species.

In a sense, though, with *Fringe*, these inaccuracies aren't really what we should be focusing on. *Fringe* does not approach science fiction in a traditional way, and it is at its best when exploring the impossible, new discoveries, humanity's capacity to eradicate itself with technology, and the responsibilities we have to curtail potential catastrophe. As such, its smartest, edgiest episodes deal with categorizing infectious diseases in new ways, such as in attacks carried out by soldiers of the other side, darkly clever in their execution and innovation. It takes liberties with the very definition of infectious diseases, elevating illness and infections to an interdimensional level, to the point that the idea of infection may even lay at the heart of our Universe's very survival.

---

1   "5 Deadliest Pandemics in History," www.neatorama.com.

Infectious Disease in *Fringe*

What is an infectious disease? Also referred to as communicable or transmissible diseases, infectious diseases are defined as illnesses with clinical symptoms arising from infection by, presence of, and growth of a pathogen (a category that includes viruses, bacteria, fungi, protozoa, etc.) in a host organism. This would include, but not be limited to, everything from viral infections such as influenza and the common cold, to bacterial infections such as MRSA and *Clostridium difficile*, to rare but frightening hemorraghic viruses like Ebola and Marburg. Definitions of infectious diseases have evolved in modern times to include bioengineered weapons, chemicals, and any agents that can "infect" an organism, as a traditional disease would, an idea that the writers of *Fringe* have pushed to the scientific limit thematically.

When it comes to the show, there are four major categories into which we may divide infectious diseases—traditional infections (which include mass death by chemical and biological warfare), designer infectious diseases, "fringe" infectious diseases of a more nebulous origin, and interuniverse sickness, a theme that brokers a commentary on the broader meaning of disease in general.

Traditional Infectious Diseases

The most common kind of infectious disease seen in science fiction is biological. Think of movies such as *Outbreak*, *28 Days*

Later, and *The Andromeda Strain* (all involving viruses or the plague), or, more recently, the hit show *The Walking Dead*, in which an unknown biological infection has wiped out the majority of the Earth and turned survivors into zombies. In *Fringe*, we see such a straightforward example of biological infection in "What Lies Below." But we also see a few other more traditional biologically based viral infections. In real life, these are far deadlier than their chemical counterparts (which we'll discuss in a moment), but on the show are often tinged with cheeky humor. In the season-one episode "Bound" (1-11) a college professor hired by a CDC task force to fight potential epidemics choked to death on a large single cell of the naso-pharyngitis virus—the common cold. If the idea of FBI agents chasing down a slimy giant rhinovirus all over a university auditorium doesn't elicit a chuckle, one doesn't have a sense of science humor. In the episode "The Transformation" (1-13), a man aboard a plane literally transformed into a Sasquatch-like spiky creature and killed everyone onboard. (Seriously, what do the writers of *Fringe* have against airplanes?) Walter hypothesized that the man was killed by the designer virus of a bioterror cell, a virus that literally rearranged his DNA in real time. Points for laughs aside, clearly these plot points are not realistic. For instance, to date, the largest recorded single-celled self-perpetuating organisms include the ostrich egg and the green algae *Caulerpa*, with some subtropical species growing cells up to a meter long.

The ideas underlying "Bound" and "The Transformation," however, are worthy of note. Viruses are, in fact, amazingly adaptive and clever microorganisms, much to the dismay of scientists and doctors everywhere. Their adaptability is part of what makes them such effective infectious agents. Viruses as common as influenza and the collective nasopharyngitis family, and as lethal as HIV, Ebola, Marburg, and the like, are constantly evolving and changing their composition (even, in some cases, postinfection), making cures unlikely at best, and making the viruses dangerous weapons if altered or manipulated (see the section on designer infectious diseases below).

While the organisms in "Bound" and "The Transformation" were fairly inert and not known to be homicidal toward epidemiologists, the field of genetic engineering is advancing at a very fast pace. A team of researchers in England, for example, has recently undertaken experiments[2] to turn a type of slime mold into functioning robots, capable of picking objects up and even assembling them. Likewise, DNA transformation, now routinely used in bacterial molecular biology, is still a fairly complex process in higher-order organisms. The best examples of such rapid DNA change due to a virus are DNA tumor viruses and RNA retroviruses.[3] In both, the virus takes up residence in a cell, now "transformed," and begins to change properties within that cell, including increasing the rate of growth and turning off programmed cell death—two hallmarks of cancer. Wholescale DNA transformation is still, thankfully, a science-fiction concept, but it is an important theme within the show, most obviously with the group of Others known as shape-shifters.

Many, if not most, of the scientific plots of *Fringe* center around bioengineered phenomena like the ones in "Bound"

---

2   "Slimebot: Programming the Single-Cell Organism," www.computerweekly. com.

3   Richard C. Hunt, "Oncogenic Viruses," pathmicro.med.sc.edu.

and "The Transformation"—the applications and adaptations of novel experimental discoveries for nefarious supernatural aims. It's not surprising, then, that the exploration of infectious diseases on the show pushes ethical and technological boundaries, in no area more germane to our current times than synthetic chemical weapons. In the opening minutes of the *Fringe* pilot, a terrorist and former Massive Dynamic employee injected himself with a mysterious chemical, which within minutes resulted in a terrifying, Ebola-like plague that killed the entire plane. In the later episode "The Cure" (1-6), a young woman dosed with a time-release radiation pill for a very rare autoimmune disease acted as a radiation emitter and killed an entire diner full of people by literally microwaving their brains.

There are several advantages and disadvantages of chemical warfare agents,[4] as proposed in these *Fringe* plots. As noted in the discussion of "What Lies Below," one large disadvantage is the inability of chemical weapons to kill on the same massive scale as biological or nuclear agents; most estimates describe the casualty capacity as ranging from the hundreds to just a few thousand. Also, effective means of delivery for these agents is far more difficult to arrange than for biological agents. They are deadly in small areas (such as the 1995 Tokyo sarin gas subway attack[5] or the *Fringe* airplane attack), but larger areas reduce casualties significantly due to the wider dispersal of disease particles, which often need close contact for transmission. They

---

4   For further reading on chemical warfare, visit www.jewishvirtuallibrary.org.

5   Jonathan B. Tucker, "The Future of Chemical Weapons," www.thenewat lantis.com.

are far cheaper to acquire than biological agents (and sometimes come ready-made without further need for assembly or modification), but more often than not require the kind of batch laboratory synthetic preparation unavailable to terrorist organizations. As such, the use of large-scale chemical weaponry of this nature in the real world has thankfully been rare.[6] The capacity to imagine, synthesize, and utilize it, however, is not.

Designer Infectious Diseases

If the large-scale *Fringe* attack plots fall shorter on realism than ambition, episodes dealing with small-scale, or designer, weapons development are rooted in frightening scientific possibilities and ongoing real-life research. Designer viruses have become a rapidly emerging scientific discipline,[7] and laboratory experimentation has resulted in "designer" viruses capable of attacking deadly hospital bacteria,[8] cancer,[9] and even tiny nanoparticle "smart" adenoviruses that act as drug delivery particles.[10]

One designer weapon features in the best scientifically written episode to date, "The Bishop Revival" (2-14), in which

6 Gerard J. Fitzgerald, "Chemical Warfare and Medical Response During World War I," www.redorbit.com.

7 "Sessions Cover 'Designer Viruses', Spread of Global Disease," www.aps.org.

8 "Students Use Designer Virus to Attack Bacterial Drug Resistance," www.eurekalert.org.

9 "Viruses as Anticancer Drugs," *Trends in Pharmacological Sciences* 28 (2007).

10 "Designer Adenoviruses for Nanomedicine and Nanodiagnostics," *Trends Biotechnol* 4 (2009).

a Nazi used research papers he stole from Dr. Bishop's father to tailor chemical weapons to target specific genetic traits—only Jewish people at a wedding, for example, or only people with brown eyes at a coffee shop. Not in a million years? Think again. On the heels of major gene therapy advances in the 1990s, as well as the whole-scale study of genes (genomics) and the proteins they encode (proteomics), research into specific cellular pathways, plus large-scale genetic changes incurred with exposure to chemical warfare agents,[11] might lead to the potential development of genetically engineered biological weapons. The history of targeting ethnic groups is long and complex, and mostly involves the exposure of nonimmune groups to smallpox and bubonic plague. In "The Bishop Revival," the scientist attached specific DNA markers (eye color, racial specificity) to a chemical molecule. In reality, the ripest candidates for use in creating targeted DNA-based weapons would be already-existing viruses such as Ebola or Machupo coupled with the DNA of a specific ethnic or racial group. Likewise, scientists could target even larger groups of people by rendering innocuous viruses such as smallpox active, or target smaller subsets of populations by inactivating essential immune proteins endemic to certain ethnic groups.

Bioterrorism communities and human rights groups have voiced anxiety over the potential uses of these biological agents in warfare and combat.[12] Unlike fast-acting wipeout agents such

---

11 "Genomics and Proteomics in Chemical Warfare Agent Research," *Toxicology Letters* 3 (2010).

12 Ronald Bailey, "Open Secrets of Biosecurity," http://reason.com. "Is All Fair in Biological Warfare? The Controversy Over Genetically Engineered Biological Weapons," *Journal of Medical Ethics* 35 (2009).

as the chemical exposure in the *Fringe* pilot or the Ebola-like hemorrhagic fever in "The Cure," designer weapons could impact everything from reproductive capacity to the practice of reverse gene therapy, or even indigenous plants and animals, affecting a certain area's food supply. Such insidious acts could take years to manifest, prompting concern that the Human Genome Research project could be abused[13] to these ends without manifesting deleterious results for a long time.

An earlier episode, "The Ghost Network" (1-3), featured another example of a nonnatural infection used as a weapon. In it, the team investigated a man who was able to predict major world incidents before they happened, including the collective attacks comprising "The Pattern"; he was, in essence, "infected" with imagery. Dr. Bishop's examination revealed the presence of organometallic compounds in his brain—specifically, an iridium-based radioactive compound—that had effectively turned him into a kind of designer weapon: a human receiver for thoughts. Bishop's research with erstwhile partner William Bell postulated the presence of a specialized wave spectrum for human thought called "the ghost network."

Naturally occurring metal-containing compounds have a widespread indispensable presence in human physiology, from the iron in hemoglobin to the zinc in the enzyme carbonic anhydrase to copper in the protein group hepatocupreins.[14] One of the earliest written records of medicinal treatments, the "Ebers"

---

13   V. Sarich and F. Miele, *Race: The Realities of Human Difference* (Boulder, Colorado: Westview Press, 2005).

14   Alaa S. Abd-El-Aziz, Charles E. Carraher Jr., Charles U. Pittman Jr., John E. Sheats, and Martel Zeldin, eds, "Macromolecules Containing Metal and Metal-Like Elements," *Biomedical Applications* 3 (2004).

papyrus, dated at around 1500 B.C., describes more than 800 compounds containing metals, many of which are still in use today, ranging from antiseptics, bactericides, and fungicides to antidepressants, Parkinson's therapy, and antitumor agents, among others. More recently, iridium-containing compounds have found implementation in the detection of and experimental therapy for a brain tumor class called glioblastomas,[15] and as soft tissue markers for living cells in bioimaging applications such as CT scans and MRIs.

The scenario portrayed in "The Ghost Network" may also sprout legs in modern biophysics research, where sputtered iridium oxide (SIROF) has been shown to be a candidate for use both in neural stimulation and as a recording electrode.[16] Recently, a model for an implanted brain biosensor was developed that uses an activated iridium disk electrode,[17] which has led to the development of a bona fide implantable recording electrode[18] similar to the one in "The Ghost Network." While these devices are likely the future of prostheses, spinal cord injury, and stroke treatments, as well as treatment for neurological disorders, if they were placed in

---

15 "Functional IrIII Complexes and Their Applications," *Advanced Materials* 13 (2010).

16 S. F. Cogan, J. Ehrlich, T. D. Plante, and R. Van Wagenen, "Penetrating Microelectrode Arrays with Low-Impedance Sputtered Iridium Oxide Electrode Coatings," *Engineering in Medicine and Biology Society* (2009).

17 Z. M. Zain, R. D. O'Neill, J. P. Lowry, K. W. Pierce, M. Tricklebank, A. Dewa, and S. Ab Ghani, "Development of an Implantable D-Serine Biosensor for In Vivo Monitoring Using Mammalian D-Amino Acid Oxidase on a Poly (O-Phenylenediamine) and Nafion-Modified Platinum-Iridium Disk Electrode," *Biosens Bioelectron* 6 (2010).

18 S. F. Cogan, "Neural Stimulation and Recording Electrodes," *Annual Review of Biomedical Engineering* 10 (2008).

the wrong hands, or perfected in a laboratory with the limitless funds and ambition of Massive Dynamic, one has to wonder if any one of us could be turned into a walking receiver. After all, Massive Dynamic's wide-scale technology and research (or Walternate's research labs on the other side) is often either at the heart of, or in some way associated with, the show's infectious diseases and the damage they cause.

Pushing the Boundaries of Infectious Disease

One of my favorite aspects of *Fringe*, and one of its greatest services for science, is the episodes that push the limits and definitions of the very concept they are centered around. What ultimately defines an infectious disease? What are the boundaries of virology? And is something "infectious" if it doesn't enter your body through traditional communicable disease pathways (i.e., via inhalation, contact with the eyes or mouth, contact with an open wound, etc.)?

"The Ghost Network" is one of these. In another, my favorite episode, "The No-Brainer" (1-12), a disgruntled computer engineer created a hypnotic computer virus that liquefied the brains of its victims through audiovisual hyperstimulation. The program literally fried its viewers' brains. Most medical cases of brain liquefication (referred to as colliquative necrosis) occur due to what's discovered postmortem to be bacterial or fungal infections that kill the cells that comprise the central nervous system. Medical research into brain liquefication has not yielded definitive causes, and recorded cases are few and far between.[19] But this brilliantly constructed episode does beg asking the question: What can a computer virus do? What physiological damage can one do through a computer? With the average world denizen spending over sixty hours a month online (equivalent to thirty straight days a year!)[20] and our ever increasing dependency on computers for daily personal and professional life, exploring the potential for computers to act as twenty-first century disease vessels is an interesting hypothetical exercise.

Another interesting application? The idea of infecting people with emotions or through kinetic energy. In the episode "Bad Dreams" (1-17), Agent Dunham realized she was sharing dreams with a fellow experimental cortexiphan subject who was able to control people through thoughts and emotions. At one point, her male counterpart led a group of people to a rooftop to commit suicide—a kind of sleepwalking epidemic. In a later episode, "Olivia. In the Lab. With the Revolver" (2-17), another cortexaphan victim suffering from late-stage cancer killed off other cortexaphan kids one by one by giving them an aggressive, accelerated cancer via energy transfer with the touch of his hand. It's a scientific fact that cancer cannot be contracted simply through touch, but this cluster of cases feeds into a significant theme on *Fringe*: the idea of chaos, disorder, and loss of control through infection.

---

19 "Cardiac Beriberi: Morphological Findings in Two Fatal Cases," *Diagnostic Pathology* 1 (2011).

20 "How the World Spends Its Time Online," www.visualeconomics.com.

Interuniverse Infection

Beyond specific episodic examples, *Fringe* makes a more extensive overall statement on the destructive potential of diseases. We have heard Walter say on a number of occasions that a person is not able to withstand travel between the two universes multiple times, and that each trip not only makes the traveler sicker, but also that very universe itself.

Walter, Olivia, Peter, and William Bell can defy every law of physics and astronomy to cross over to the other side but cannot ignore the debilitating side effects that ravage their earthly bodies. The other cortexiphan subjects who crossed over with Walter, Olivia, and Bell in the season-two finale, for example, didn't survive long after their crossing. And it was Walter's original crossing that led to the instabilities we see in the fabric of both universes. Here, the acting infectious agent is interuniverse travel itself, with contact between universes acting as the disease vector, or transmission agent.

Most tellingly, the show itself uses terminology associated with disease in discussing these events: the Fringe Division Over There calls its use of amber resin *quarantine*. By isolating these fringe event sites, they are able to stop their spread. Our world seems not far behind—though the pathogen in our world's case *more often* seems to be those from the other side, here to cause intentional damage. But when faced with a fringe event similar to the other universe's in "6B" (3-14), Broyles and Walter consider, though eventually reject, similar quarantine methods. (This sparks an important topic for consideration in our world, as well: when it comes to social quarantine methods, what is morally and politically acceptable during pandemic states?)

So the picture we get of the alternate universe is of a world fighting for its life against spreading disease; a place that is fundamentally sick, fighting the illness that threatens its life the only way it knows how—and, as when our bodies fight infection, its attempts to save its own life, led by Walternate, may cause it as much harm as good. In fact, Walternate's plan to destroy our Universe—the infecting agent—ends with his own being destroyed (at least the first time around).

High-Concept Epidemiology

Large-scale infection is perhaps the most frightening scientific topic that entertainment can broach, partially because it remains so scary in real life. With infectious diseases, especially, comes a loss of control and order, an important thread connecting the two contrasting universes of *Fringe*'s world. In almost every episode containing a virus plot, a man-made or designer virus has gotten or is about to get into the wrong hands.

Nearly every topic explored on the show is meant to titillate and unnerve in small doses, while seamlessly plugging into the larger overall picture of the powerful capacity and potential for destruction posed by unfettered science and technology. And the show explores infectious diseases the same way it does other scientific concepts—in terms of the ability, whether in our Universe or the other, to use it as a weapon.

Perhaps the most surprising element of the show is that pandemics, disfiguring infections, and incurable diseases aren't used *more* often, especially given the show's ambitious incorporation of diseases on a wide scale. After all, mind control, alternate universes, and mysterious murders are all scary concepts. But otherworldly diseases that we have no cure for and have never even defined? That is truly petrifying. Moreover, our own technological prowess, including in the area of bioengineered disease, continually threatens to outpace our ethics. *Fringe* dares to ask us what the limits of science should be, whose hands this technology belongs in, and what responsibility powerful conglomerate corporations such as Massive Dynamic have to keep that technology in check.

Because the weapons of earthly biology are the most powerful and dangerous of all, *Fringe* suggests we should continue our explorations only in the smartest way possible: with supreme caution.

JOVANA J. GRBIĆ PhD, is the editor and creative director of ScriptPhD.com, specializing in creative content consulting and development for science and technology in entertainment, media, and advertising. She tweets as @ScriptPhD and can be found on Facebook.com/ScriptPhD. She received her BA in physical chemistry from Northwestern University, a PhD in oncogenomics from The Scripps Research Institute, and completed a fellowship in infectious diseases at The UCLA School of Public Health.

THE FRINGES OF NEUROTECHNOLOGY

BRENDAN ALLISON

Creators of science-fiction works are often outwardly proud of the predictive nature of science fiction over the decades—at how many of the situations, physical phenomena, and devices have come to fruition after first being described in a work of sci-fi. The idea that an interface can be implanted within a human brain to control a device or machine is nothing new to science fiction. Just as the level of technological sophistication of the communicators from the original *Star Trek*, originally a futuristic sci-fi gadget, has already been far surpassed in the real world, what's possible today in the field of brain-computer interfaces (BCIs) will likely surprise you. Brendan Allison, PhD, examines how BCIs, and the field of neurotechnology, are presented in science fiction—and in particular *Fringe*—and details for us what is, and is not, the state of the art.

> "I think it's time for some intracranial penetration."
>
> –WALTER BISHOP, "THE GHOST NETWORK" (1-3)

> "The brain *is* a computer . . . It's an organic computer; it can
> be hijacked like any other."
>
> –WALTER BISHOP, "OF HUMAN ACTION" (2-7)

F ans of *Fringe* won't be surprised to hear that neurotechnology, an increasingly popular research field at the intersection of technology and the brain, has also become quite a popular topic in today's sci-fi. The mysteries of the human brain and its relation to technology have provided some of the show's most memorable moments, from the retrieval of Walter's surgically stolen memories to Peter, Walter, and William Bell's journey through Olivia's brain. However, while we can all recognize when something involves the brain and technology, the term "neurotechnology" can actually prove pretty tricky to define.

There are many different definitions out there, but I'll use the definition from the University of Frieburg, a well-established research group. Their definition divides neurotechnology into two types of technologies:

(I) technical and computational tools that measure and analyze chemical and electrical signals in the nervous system, be it the brain or nerves in the limbs. These may be used to identify the properties of nervous activity, understand how the brain works, diagnose pathological conditions, or control external devices (neuroprostheses, "brain machine interfaces").

(II) technical tools to interact with the nervous system to change its activity, for example to restore sensory input such as with cochlear implants to restore hearing or deep brain stimulation to stop tremor and treat other pathological conditions.[1]

In short, part (I) refers to devices that *read from* the brain (such as an EEG, MEG, or MRI), and part (II) describes devices that *write to* the brain (such as a cochlear implant or deep brain stimulator).

The area I work in, and in which Walter Bishop sometimes dabbles, is a specialized kind of neurotechnology called brain-computer interfaces, or BCIs. A BCI is explicitly defined as a device with four characteristics: it must (1) rely on direct measures of brain activity, (2) work in real time, (3) provide feedback to the user, and (4) rely on voluntary, intentional control.[2] (Therefore, devices that write to the brain or rely on *involuntary or unintentional* signals, though they are still neurotechnology, are not BCIs.)

Neither BCIs nor other types of brain reading and writing devices are especially new. For example, deep brain implants

---

1 "Neurotechnology: A Definition," www.neurotechnology.uni-freiburg.de.

2 J. R. Wolpaw, N. Birbaumer, D. J. McFarland, G. Pfurtscheller, and T. M. Vaughan, "Brain–Computer Interfaces for Communication and Control," *Clinical Neurophysiology* 113 (2002).

G. Pfurtscheller, B. Z. Allison, C. Brunner, G. Bauernfeind, T. Solis Escalante, R. Scherer, T. O. Zander, G. Müller-Putz, C. Neuper, and N. Birbaumer, "The Hybrid BCI," *Frontiers in Neuroscience* 4 (2010).

have been used for decades and have helped many people with Parkinson's disease and other movement disorders, chronic pain, and other conditions.

Stories about neurotechnology are not new either. They have been popular with sci-fi fans for decades; *Neuromancer* and the cyberpunk subgenre are grounded in the future of BCIs, and all five Star Trek series addressed neurotechnology many times. Technology used for mind reading and mind melding show up in *The Matrix, Strange Days, Total Recall, Brainstorm,* and *X-Men,* and mind control facilitated by technological innovation has been a staple of sci-fi for a long time. In fact, the fascination with brain-computer interactions is so prevalent in sci-fi that you could even name a subgenre after it: bci-fi. What is new—and sudden—is the way neurotechnology has seized popular attention, not just among the stereotypical bespectacled lonely males who can recite Monty Python and Maxwell's equations in hexadecimal code, but through more mainstream shows like *Fringe.*

Fringe is well named. On the one hand, I doubt I'm surprising or offending many fans by noting that many of the show's plots and devices are quite far from reality. On the other hand, like most good fiction, *Fringe* is obviously inspired by reality. Often, I've recognized similarities to real-world research studies that may have gotten the writers' neurons firing. But the show usually adds some new twist involving neurotechnology or the people who use it that leads to a bizarre, violent, and harrowing inciting incident. Our task here will be to separate the truth from the fiction, the better to highlight *Fringe*'s creativity.

A *Fringe* Case Study

Let's look briefly at the season-two episode "Of Human Action," where a troubled teenager named Tyler developed the ability to make others do anything he wanted, just by popping some pills from Massive Dynamic's version of a PEZ dispenser. These powerful drugs were part of a neurotechnological experiment: they were developed to amplify the brain waves of military pilots so that they could use a new hands-free navigation system to steer planes using only their thoughts (as picked up via electrodes in a helmet). Tyler, however, used the pills to fake his own kidnapping, hypnotizing random adults to commit criminal and even suicidal actions.

This might seem like pure fantasy—the sort of stuff you'd see in X-Men movies or *The Lawnmower Man*—but the ideas are actually based on some real-life developments. Which of these claims are true?

A) The air force has developed a noninvasive BCI that uses sensors placed in helmets to let pilots control aircraft.

B) Drugs can enhance some of the brain's EEG patterns and make them more recognizable to a mind-reading device.

C) Hypnosis can change the alpha waves of the brain.

The answer? All of them—with some explanation. As far as option A is concerned, the USAF developed such a BCI over ten years ago.[3] However, pilots could only use it to bank aircraft, not

---

3 M. Middendorf, G. McMillan, G. Calhoun, and K. S. Jones, "Brain–Computer Interfaces Based on Steady-State Visual Evoked Response," *IEEE Transactions on Rehabilitation Engineering* 8 (2000).

perform more complex tasks as implied in the *Fringe* episode. The device was noninvasive, and several groups funded by the US Military and others have worked on brain-wave sensors that could be placed in helmets or elsewhere.[4] Those of us in BCI research are still very actively researching practical electrodes— by which I mean electrodes that do not require electrode gel, as conventional electrodes do. (Conventional electrodes require rubbing the scalp under each electrode and squirting some electrode gel to get a good connection. The process is safe and painless, but wastes time and tends to be messy.) Companies like Neurosky, Emotiv, g.tec, TMSi, and even Mattel and Hasbro have begun selling BCIs with practical electrodes, primarily to play simple games. Remarkably, Dr. Thomas Sullivan from Neurosky told me they have sold over a million of their BCI chips, and primarily in systems meant for the general public—a much wider distribution than just a few years ago.

You can gather evidence of option B just by drinking your morning coffee (at least if you happen to have an EEG recording device handy). When you give someone caffeine, or any stimulant, his EEG patterns might become more recognizable to a

---

4 F. Popescu, S. Fazli, Y. Badower, B. Blankertz, and K. R. Müller, "Single Trial Classification of Motor Imagination Using 6 Dry EEG Electrodes," PLoS One 2 (2007).

L. J. Trejo, N. J. McDonald, R. Matthews, and B. Z. Allison, "Experimental Design and Testing of a Multimodal Cognitive Overload Classifier," *Automated Cognition International Conference* (2007).

C. T. Lin, L. D. Liao, Y. H. Liu, I. J. Wang, B. S. Lin, and J. Y. Chang, "Novel Dry Polymer Foam Electrodes for Long-Term EEG Measurement," *IEEE Transactions on Biomedical Engineering* 5 (2011).

A. Luo, and T. J. Sullivan, "A User-Friendly SSVEP-Based Brain-Computer Interface Using a Time-Domain Classifier," *Journal of Neural Engineering* 2 (2010).

recording device—though so far, caffeine does not seem to affect BCI performance.[5] Whether other drugs can enhance BCI performance, we don't know yet, but it is of interest to us—check again in five years, and I suspect we'll have more solid results.

Option C, which Walter commented on only in passing, is also true—in fact, it dates back to what would have been Walter's early research days. We've known for decades that hypnosis can change alpha waves, as well as theta and some other brain-wave patterns.[6]

So far, everything we've explored in "Of Human Action" was based on real events. Of course, then came the *Fringe* twist. The pills didn't just make Tyler's brain waves easier to pick up; he could use them to control other people's minds. Fortunately, this is quite impossible for many reasons (discussed in the mind control section below). Another bit of fiction? Dr. Bishop commented that resisting mind control can leave lesions on the surface of the brain. Though this helped make for engaging drama, it had no basis in reality.

(As a side note, about eight minutes into this episode, Dr. Bishop mentioned a neurobiology conference he once attended

---

5 B. Z. Allison, D. Valbuena, T. Lueth, A. Teymourian, I. Volosyak, and A. Gräser, "BCI Demographics: How Many (And What Kinds of) People Can Use an SSVEP BCI?" *Transactions on Neural Systems and Rehabilitation Engineering* 18 (2010).

6 P. London, J. T. Hart, and M. P. Leibovitz, "EEG Alpha Rhythms and Susceptibility to Hypnosis," *Nature* 219 (1968).

W. Larbig, T. Elbert, W. Lutzenberger, B. Rockstroh, G. Schnerr, and N. Birbaumer, "EEG and Slow Brain Potentials During Anticipation and Control of Painful Stimulation," *Electroencephalogrophy and Clinical Neurophysiology* 53 (1982).

B. Z. Allison, A. Vankov, J. Overton, M. Cassarino, and J. A. Pineda, "Selective Attention to Tactile Stimuli During Hypnosis and Waking Conditions, *Society for Neuroscience* 23 (1997).

in Berlin. There actually was a large international BCI conference in Berlin in 2009, and one of the speakers was Dr. Niels
Birbaumer, one of the giants of our BCI research community.
His talk is available online at http://videolectures.net/bbci09_
birbaumer_bip/. You can judge for yourself whether there are
any similarities between the Doctors B.)

So the writers take a seemingly innocuous or even actively
benevolent scientific advancement, and then imagine what
would happen if something went wrong—if neurons *didn't* have
checks and balances, if sleep therapy induced instead of
prevented nightmares, if a hands-free aircraft navigation
became hands-free *people* navigation. This MO—a little bit of
reality and a lot of fiction—makes for compelling stories. And
knowing exactly which is which lets us appreciate what the
Fringe writers do even more. So let's look a little deeper at
neurotechnology, both as it exists in the real world and as it's
reflected in *Fringe*.

Mind Reading

Current brain computer technology is often compared to mind
reading: we have many ways to find out what's happening in the
brain, from MRIs to EEGs to X-rays. But even the most advanced
BCIs and other neurotechnology are not literal mind-reading
devices. That is, you cannot simply think any word, image, or
tune and have it appear on a monitor. We've tried. We keep
trying. We are still not close.

"Downloading" your experiences onto a computer or someone
else's brain is a popular theme in *Fringe*. It was introduced in the

very first episode with the prospect of "interrogating" John Scott's dead brain (which was apparently feasible because he had been dead for *five* hours, not six—that six-hour limit doesn't really occupy real BCI scientists much). In "Grey Matters" (2-10), an episode whose title warns you to expect some serious breaches of the Hippocratic oath, pieces of Bishop's brain were removed and put into other people's brains (though a brain reading a brain is arguably not neurotechnology, since the brain is not a device). The poor victims went crazy downloading just a smidgen of Bishop (perhaps because even that tiny amount had enough stored drugs to make three victims trip for fourteen years). At the end of "Os" (3-16), William Bell's consciousness was "downloaded" into Olivia's body after his death using "soul magnets."

In other examples of using technology to read human thoughts and memories, Dr. Bishop "read" the last image a dead woman saw by scanning her optic nerve (which, he said, would have been absurd but for the fact that she had relaxants in her system that "froze" the image) in "The Same Old Story" (1-2); Dr. Nayak could experience other people's dreams by eavesdropping with an evil BCI in "Dream Logic" (2-5); and in "Unearthed" (2-11), Dr. Bishop noticed that a murder victim, Andrew Rusk, had taken over a teenage girl by looking at what seemed to be only one very noisy channel of EEG data. These are exciting, haunting ideas, and so it is understandable that they led to good stories. But they aren't possible.

Here is about where we are today: BCIs work by detecting certain brain activity patterns associated with voluntary mental activities. Unfortunately, most of the things people think, feel, want, or perceive do not produce patterns of brain activity that we can discriminate. Different thoughts, feelings, desires, and perceptions do reflect different brain states, but we lack the neuroimaging and signal processing technology to distinguish nearly all of them. Therefore, BCI research has had to proceed so far based on the relatively few distinct brain states that we can identify. The most common BCI approaches rely on imagined movement or visual attention, not because these are the most natural or obvious activities to use for communication or control, but because brain states associated with some movement and visual attention tasks are the ones we know how to recognize, at least under very specific conditions.[7]

There are certainly other intentions that BCIs can read. For example, the first BCI paper published in *Nature* relied on a different approach called Slow Cortical Potential, or SCP. SCP works by reading different emotional or cognitive tasks the user can learn to perform.[8] Other BCIs rely on conventional tasks like rotating an object, imagined singing, or math.[9] But most BCIs today are based on motor imagery and visual attention.

---

7   J. R. Wolpaw, N. Birbaumer, D. J. McFarland, G. Pfurtscheller, and T. M. Vaughan, "Brain–Computer Interfaces for Communication and Control."

N. Birbaumer, and L. G. Cohen, "Brain-Computer Interfaces: Communication and Restoration of Movement in Paralysis," *The Journal of Physiology* 579 (2007).

B. Graimann, B. Z. Allison, and G. Pfurtscheller, "A Gentle Introduction to Brain–Computer Interface (BCI) Systems," *Brain-Computer Interfaces: Revolutionizing Human-Computer Interaction* (New York: Springer, 2010).

8   N. Birbaumer, N. Ghanayim, T. Hinterberger, I. Iversen, B. Kotchoubey, A. Kübler, J. Perelmouter, E. Taub, and H. Flor, "A Spelling Device for the Paralyzed," *Nature* 398 (1999).

9   J. R. Millán, F. Renkens, J. Mouriño, and W. Gerstner, "Noninvasive Brain-Actuated Control of a Mobile Robot by Human EEG," *IEEE Transactions on Biomedical Engineering* 51 (2004).

Imagined Movement BCIs

BCIs are often based on some type of imagined movement, but they can only recognize a few different signals. For example, if you think about moving your left hand, right hand, or feet, you get reliably different activity over somatomotor areas of the brain responsible for movement and touch (specifically, the areas around the central sulcus, which is located on the top of the brain and divides the frontal and parietal lobes). Imagining (or performing) left-hand movement will show up in the EEG as a reduction in "power" somewhere between 8 to 12 Hz over these areas on the right side of the brain.[10] (For reasons we only partly understand,[11] many different mental activities are correlated with 8 to 12 Hz power changes. For example, relaxing or closing your eyes, a common way to control simple toy BCIs, can cause an increase of 8 to 12 Hz power.) Right-hand movement produces changes over the left side, and foot movement produces activity that is most distinct over the center.

---

10 J. A. Pineda, B. Z. Allison, and A. Vankov, "The Effects of Self-Movement, Observation, and Imagination on Mu Rhythms and Readiness Potentials: Toward a Brain-Computer Interface (BCI)," *IEEE Transactions on Neural Systems and Rehabilitation Engineering* 8 (2000).

C. Neuper, M. Wörtz, and G. Pfurtscheller, "ERD/ERS Patterns Reflecting Sensorimotor Activation and Deactivation," *Progress in Brain Research* 159 (2006).

G. Pfurtscheller, and C. Neuper, "Dynamics of Sensorimotor Oscillations in a Motor Task," in *Brain-Computer Interfaces: Revolutionizing Human-Computer Interaction* (New York: Springer, 2010).

11 G. Pfurtscheller and F. H. Lopes da Silva, "Event-Related EEG/MEG Synchronization and Desynchronization: Basic Principles," *Clinical Neurophysiology* 110 (1999).

Hence, you could—by reading a subject's intended hand and foot movement—allow them to navigate a virtual environment, spell, or perform other tasks just by thinking.[12] A recent paper described a landmark achievement: people who could move a cursor in all three dimensions (left/right, up/down, and forward/ backward) with a noninvasive BCI.[13] However, this feat required dozens of hours of training, and even with training (pending further research) seems to be possible only for a small percentage of people.

Visual Attention BCIs

We can also tell if you are "paying attention" to—i.e., looking at—one item out of several items, at least if the items flicker or flash in a specific pattern (say, if the items are LEDs or images on a monitor). Specific patterns are necessary because each pattern elicits a different pattern in brain activity, and hence each pattern creates a unique signal that a BCI can distinguish.

There are two types of BCIs based on this kind of visual attention. They are named after the type of visual stimulation used,

---

12   C. Neuper, M. Wörtz, and G. Pfurtscheller, "ERD/ERS Patterns Reflecting Sensorimotor Activation and Deactivation," *Progress in Brain Research* 159 (2006).

R. Scherer, F. Lee, A. Schlogl, R. Leeb, H. Bischof, and G. Pfurtscheller, "Toward Self-Paced Brain-Computer Communication: Navigation Through Virtual Worlds," *IEEE Transactions on Biomedical Engineering* 55 (2008).

B. Z. Allison, D. Valbuena, T. Lueth, A. Teymourian, I. Volosyak, and A. Gräser, "BCI Demographics: How Many (And What Kinds of) People Can Use an SSVEP BCI?"

13   D. J. McFarland, W. A. Sarnacki, and J. R. Wolpaw, "Electroencephalographic (EEG) Control of Three-Dimensional Movement: *Journal of Neural Engineering* (2010.)

which results in different EEG patterns. The first, the P300 BCI, relies on flashing stimuli, such as a matrix of letters and numbers that each flash one at a time or in rows and columns.[14] The second, the SSVEP BCI, relies on oscillating stimuli, such as characters that each oscillate at a different frequency.[15]

BCI Limitations

There are certain limitations that restrict what's possible with all mind-reading BCIs.

First, you need a device on or in your brain. Most BCIs rely on noninvasive sensors—EEG electrodes outside the scalp.

---

14 B. Z. Allison, and J. A. Pineda, "ERPs Evoked by Different Matrix Sizes: Implications for a Brain Computer Interface (BCI) System," *IEEE Transactions on Neural Systems and Rehabilitation Engineering* 11 (2003).

  E. W. Sellers, A. Kübler, and E. Donchin, "Brain–Computer Interface Research at the University of South Florida Cognitive Psychophysiology Laboratory: The P300 Speller," *IEEE Transactions on Neural Systems and Rehabilitation Engineering* 14 (2006).

  E. W. Sellers, T. M. Vaughan, and J. R. Wolpaw, "A Brain-Computer Interface for Long-Term Independent Home Use," *Amyotrophic Lateral Sclerosis* 11 (2010).

  J. Jin, B. Z. Allison, C. Brunner, B. Wang, X. Wang, J. Zhang, C. Neuper, and G. Pfurtscheller, "P300 Chinese Input System Based on PSO-LDA," *Biomedical Engineering* 55 (2010).

15 G. Bin, X. Gao, y. Wang, B. Hong, and S. Gao, "VEP-Based Brain-Computer Interfaces: Time Frequency, and Code Modulations," *IEEE Computational Intelligence Magazine* 4 (2009).

  G. Bin, X. Gao, Y. Wang, Y Li, B. Hong and S. Gao, "A High-Speed BCI Based on Code Modulation VEP," *Journal of Neural Engineering* 2 (2011.)

  C. Brunner, B. Z. Allison, C. Altstätter, and C. Neuper, "A Comparison of Three BCIs Based on ERD, SSVEP, or a Hybrid Approach Using Both Signals," *Journal of Neural Engineering* 24 (2011).

  B. Z. Allison, J. Faller, and C. Neuper, "BCIs that Use Steady-State Visual Evoked Potentials or Slow Cortical Potentials," in *Brain-Computer Interfaces: Principles and Practice* (Oxford: Oxford University Press, 2012).

However, electrodes can also be implanted under the scalp, on the surface of the brain, or even inside the brain. Both types are referenced in the episode with the aforementioned evil doctor, Nayak: he seemed to wear an EEG-based system but also described implanting the electrodes in the thalamus. The system worn in "The Equation" also looks much like a jury-rigged field EEG system, and the lines on the monitor look very much like real EEG patterns. Before Agent Dunham went into the sensory deprivation tank in season one, she got an implant near her brain stem, though reading complex, specific actions would probably require electrodes elsewhere. (It is unclear why the brain stem is such a popular spot for futuristic neurotechnology implants—it seems to be in about the same place as the evil BCIs in *The Matrix, Space: 1999, X-Men II, Johnny Mnemonic*, and others.)

Second, you usually get a vocabulary of only a few signals, and you have to tell the user what to do to produce them. You can't just hook up a person (or corpse, like John Scott in several first-season episodes) and expect the BCI to read everything, or much of anything.

Third, an involuntary BCI is not really possible. Even if the user is somehow prevented from removing the electrode cap you've attached to his or her head, he or she could just choose not to think about moving or not pay attention to visual stimuli. In other words, it's no use on dead people—or sleeping ones. You cannot really "sneak" a brain imaging device on someone, although you could of course trick them into using one and then use it to read more than intended. For example, it's conceivable that a person might use a BCI to play a game, but an unscrupulous eavesdropper could determine his sleep cycle (which doesn't necessarily require a BCI; for some gamers, you need only look at when they aren't playing).

Moreover, even with the full cooperation of the user, you wouldn't really be able to determine anything useful to *Fringe's* stories, only that the user was alert or performing one of a few simple tasks. Right now, you can only pick up one signal at a time, though this could change with "hybrid" BCIs, which are one of my main research interests.[16] Under ideal circumstances, typical modern BCIs only allow their users to convey about twenty bits (or a few letters) per minute. Rich, detailed information that requires a high bandwidth is not imminent. For the moment, even the most active people in BCI research still write articles primarily with keyboards, not BCIs, and I doubt we'll change that in the next ten years, at minimum.

Is a Mind-Reading BCI Even Possible?

Will we ever develop technology that can read anything and everything people experience? Definitely not in our lifetimes, and it may not be possible with any technology;[17] this has been a philosophical debate for thousands of years. One of the best-known inquiries comes from Descartes, who mused about whether our experiences are real, or whether we might just be fooled by an evil demon who makes us think the outside world

---

16 B. Z. Allison, C. Brunner, V. Kaiser, G. Müller-Putz, C. Neuper, and G. Pfurtscheller, "A Hybrid Brain-Computer Interface Based on Imagined Movement and Visual Attention," *Journal of Neural Engineering* 7 (2010).

G. Pfurtscheller, and C. Neuper, "Dynamics of Sensorimotor Oscillations in a Motor Task."

C. Brunner, B. Z. Allison, C. Altstätter, and C. Neuper, "A Comparison of Three BCIs Based on ERD, SSVEP, or a Hybrid Approach Using Both Signals."

17 B. Z. Allison, "Toward Ubiquitous BCIs," in *Brain-Computer Interfaces: Revolutionizing Human-Computer Interaction* (New York: Springer, 2010).

really exists. Descartes concluded that we cannot be sure of anything except our own thoughts—hence his famous phrase "I think, therefore I am." Neurophilosophers and others still grapple with the discussion of whether we can really trust reality. Unless our very perception of what is possible is also fed to us (through something like the BCI in *The Matrix*), we can very safely say that reading a *complete* reality is impossible. (So is writing one, but we'll get to that in a minute.) On the other hand, this is not really necessary for developing helpful technology.

If a mind-reading revolution does occur, there is some work that might foreshadow possible mechanisms. In a recent study, subjects looked at the word "neuron" while lying in an fMRI scanner. If the subject stared for many seconds, the device could generally determine that they were observing the word "neuron" by decoding the activity in visual areas.[18] But an fMRI requires a huge superconducting magnet: the machine costs millions, and scanner time typically costs around $300 per hour. And its "mind reading" was not a real-time system. Moreover, the term "mind reading" seems rather grandiose when describing a system that can only detect one word, which is already known to the experimenters. Other work[19] asked subjects to listen to one of seven three-second segments of music. Based on the EEG, they could tell which of these seven pieces a listener was hearing with up to 70 percent accuracy in real time, and the article noted that it could be increased to 100 percent accuracy. Another very

---

18 Y. Miyawaki, H. Uchida, O. Yamashita, M. Sato, Y. Morito, H. C. Tanabe, N. Sadato, and Y. Kamitani, "Visual Image Reconstruction from Human Brain Acitivity using a Combination of Multiscale Local Image Decoders," *Neuron* 60 (2008)

19 Schaefer R. S., J. Farquhar, Y. Blokland, M. Sadakata, and P. Desain, "Name That Tune: Decoding Music from the Listening Brain," *Neuroimage* 56 (2011).

recent paper showed that an invasive BCI could distinguish between pairs of sounds heard by the user.

Perhaps the most promising recent story about where we are now comes from the work of old friends of mine in Albany. Gerwin Schalk, Theresa Vaughan, Jon Wolpaw, and others described new BCI systems, including research into an invasive BCI to distinguish between thirty-five different imagined words.[20] This is remarkable progress, but a long way from a "universal" BCI that can decode any thought.

Mind-Writing and Mind Control

We've established that mind reading, where possible, is a much more limited process than the one we see in *Fringe*. But there's another aspect to neurotechnology, and that's mind-*writing*—or, as often seen in bci-fi, mind "control."

In science fiction, mind-writing varies in sophistication from simply tweaking emotions or sleep cycles to completely replicating someone else's experience and/or dominating every action. It can be therapeutic or insidious, healing or controlling, voluntary or involuntary. The only real common thread is that it usually looks pretty effortless on the part of the controller. We see this in *Fringe* with Tyler, but also with Bell's control over Olivia's body, Dr. Nayak's dream manipulation, Rusk's control of the teenage girl in "Unearthed," and others. This is very common elsewhere in science fiction, as well. Borg technology in Star

---

20   Jon Hamilton, "Mind Reading: Technology Turns Thoughts into Action," www.npr.org.

Trek, for instance, relies in invasive BCIs that read and write to the brain.

However, tweaking brain activity in ways that produce specific and complex perceptions, emotions, experiences, or actions is not nearly that simple. And mind control like Tyler's, especially, is way, way beyond modern technology. But why?

Even beyond the question of how information was getting from one brain to another, there are limits on how specifically we can control neural activity. There are many ways to do this, ranging from basically turning neurons off or making them fire haphazardly to making an established specific network of neurons fire in a totally novel way. If you want to simply prevent an area of the mind from working, you have lots of options. Simply cooling a region of the brain can shut down function, at least for a while, without any serious or permanent effects. Damaging brain tissue would also prevent it from working, but that's of course more permanent. To cause specific behaviors (such as shooting other policemen) you need more than simple deactivation. You need to make the brain do something different. To accomplish this—to actually *alter* brain activity—you need to make neurons fire in specific patterns.

Neurons fire on their own every day; every conscious act you perform (and many other functions you're totally unaware of) is triggered by the firing of neurons. Just making neurons fire, or making them fire more, is also relatively easy. In "The No-Brainer" (1-12), a computer virus made home PCs play a movie clip designed to kill people by liquefying their brains. Dr. Bishop explained that it involved "a complex combination of visual and subsonic aural stimuli ingeniously designed to amplify the electrical impulses of the brain, trapping it in an endless loop." The "electrical impulses" Walter was referring to are the signals between neurons, and they can in fact be made to fire more than they otherwise would, even from the outside of the brain. Television shows have produced seizures in the past, through a mechanism somewhat like the phenomenon Bishop describes—excessive neural activity.

Luckily, though, the "endless loop" from that episode was just a cute metaphor. American culture loves the notion that bad programming can rot your brain—and maybe it can. Not literally and instantly, though. The brain has numerous mechanisms to prevent this kind of wildfire explosion of neural activity. Many neurons have an inhibitory feedback system that releases inhibitory neurotransmitters if the neurons themselves, or other neurons around them, become too active. This helps to prevent seizures and other problems. (Also, even if a seizure *is* induced, even serious seizures are not nearly as bad as complete brain liquification.)

Brain meltdown still won't trigger any specific actions, however, such as shooting a gun or speaking a sentence. Simply overstimulating the brain's neurons could lead to seizure, brain damage, or death. While these might be appealing goals to a mad scientist or a soulless executive, if you want a specific reaction, you need to send a specific signal, either via electrical, magnetic, or chemical means.

There are multiple ways to send such signals, but the most direct method is something invasive, such as implants or neurostimulators, and invasive stimulation methods are prominent in *Fringe*. In the real world, deep brain stimulation (DBS), for example, stimulates the brain through electrical means and is a common and effective technique to reduce symptoms of

Parkinson's disease. Doctors implant a neurostimulator into the basal ganglia, a region heavily involved in movement and production of dopamine, a neurotransmitter that is depleted in Parkinson's disease. A deep brain stimulator can stimulate neurons in some basal ganglia regions like the globus pallidus and subthalamic nucleus, which does not cure the disease but, by encouraging the production of additional dopamine, can reduce symptoms and dependence on medication.

In one famous paper in *Nature*, researchers used invasive electric stimulators to "control" rats' behavior.[21] They implanted electrodes into three regions of a rat's brain: the right and left primary somatosensory areas, which are responsible for the sensation of touch on the left and right whiskers, and the medial forebrain bundle (MFB), which is critical in reinforcement learning. The researchers stimulated the left or right whisker areas, then (if the rat turned left or right) provided a "reward" by stimulating the MFB. The rats quickly learned to turn left or right and would also move forward if you stimulated the MFB alone. After some training, they could be guided through a series of tasks and even moved through bright open areas, which rats typically avoid. Humans have more or less the same areas; our "whisker cortex" is just the part of the primary somatosensory cortex that responds to touching the face. But the effects are limited to just a few simple behaviors and must be developed over time. The control isn't instantaneous.

Invasive chemical means have also been employed in animal research to change the brain and affect behavior. By putting a

---

21 S. K. Talwar, S. Xu, E. S. Hawley, S. A. Weiss, K. A. Moxon, and J. K. Chapin, "Rat Navigation Guided by Remote Control," *Nature* 417 (2002).

device called a cannula—essentially a tube—into the brain and sending chemicals to specific brain regions, researchers can directly affect neuron behavior. This technique can be very effective for studying precisely how neurotransmitters work or how different chemicals affect different regions, but using it to control specific actions would be quite difficult.

Not every mind-writing strategy requires invasive means. There are ways to directly influence the chemical composition of the brain noninvasively as well, such as giving people drugs. This technique is, of course, Dr. Bishop's favorite, especially when it comes to affecting his own brain chemistry. However, he is far from the first person to explore the fringes of drug effects. And if people could control others' minds or perform similarly fantastic feats by taking lots of LSD, then some shivering old hippie on Haight would rule the world by now.

Pyschoactive drugs were put to a more insidious use in "The Dreamscape" (1-9). Victims were tricked by a hallucinogen produced by frogs into becoming so scared, or so convinced of some horrific fate, that they actually produced physical symptoms, such as trauma from hallucinated thugs or cuts from a thousand butterflies. This seems to be based on a couple real stories. Many people have heard examples of spontaneous injury, such as stigmata, or even spontaneous combustion. "Voodoo death," in which people become so afraid that they die, is nothing new. Similarly, there has often been enthusiasm for hypnosis, drugs, or other techniques that can help people instantly heal themselves or produce other dramatic physical changes. But these examples are fairly far removed from people suddenly developing massive and fatal physical trauma because they think they are being attacked by ghost thugs or evil mechanical butterflies. Drugs are also notoriously nonspecific, since they travel all over the brain, in different concentrations, and have different effects on different areas.

Electroshock treatment, a very old technique with some benefits for persons with mental disorders, is a fairly dramatic noninvasive way to alter the brain, but the effects are too broad to be truly useful. Newer (and rapidly developing) methods like transcranial magnetic stimulation (TMS) and transcranial direct current stimulation (TCDS) can also make neurons fire, or inhibit them, or change how they fire to influence behavior. Both of these approaches are noninvasive and involve electro-magnetic fields outside of the head. These approaches have gained a lot of attention recently within the neuroscience commu-nity, producing some promising results for treating depression, obsessive-compulsive disorder, and other conditions.[22] (Disclaimer: I invented a range of neurotechnologies based on direct elec-trical stimulation of the brain [both invasive and noninvasive], which could influence depression, fatigue, and many other func-tions, so I'm pretty biased here.[23])

However, even new and relatively precise noninvasive methods still cannot target individual neurons, or even small groups of

---

22   M. S. George, "Transcranial Magnetic Stimulation for the Treatment of Depression," *Expert Review of Neurotherapeutics* 10 (2010).

     W. Wang, J. L. Collinger, M. A. Perez, E. C. Tyler-Kabara, L. G. Cohen, N. Birbaumer, S. W. Brose, A. B. Schwartz, M. L. Boninger, and D. J. Weber, "Neural Interface Technology for Rehabilitation: Exploring and Promoting Neuroplasticity," *Physical Medicine and Rehabilization Clinics of North America* 21 (2010).

23   J. A. Pineda, and B. Z. Allison, "Method and System for a Real Time Adap-tive System for Effecting Changes in Cognitive-Emotive Profiles," *U.S. Patent Serial No. US 7,460,903* (2008).

them, which is necessary if you want to produce specific complex actions. Even invasive techniques, which can produce much more precise changes, are of limited value because we often do not know which neurons we need to influence, and how. One other drawback of invasive technologies is flexibility. Even if you know how to implant a network of stimulating electrodes that gives good control over all possible movements of a single finger, what if you want to control another finger? To produce a range of complex movements, you'd need numerous stimulating electrodes, in specific areas, capable of stimulating neurons in specific patterns.

It would probably be easier to trigger complex actions that the user does frequently. Walking is quite complex, but is also so well established that a simple command can trigger a lot of complex movements. If you want to make someone play a complex piece on the piano, it is probably much easier if you find a victim who already has spent hundreds of hours playing it.

Let's look at the complexity involved in stimulating specific neurons to get an intended result by taking the example of vision. Say you want to make someone see a tree that isn't really there. The primary visual cortex is a horribly serpentine mess, with dozens of overlapping regions that all perform different functions. These microstructures are generally smaller than a millimeter across, and twist and tangle across three dimensions. Which neurons would you stimulate to replicate a picture of a tree? And how exactly would you stimulate them, and nothing else?

There has been some work toward writing visual images directly on the eye or brain, primarily to help people who have trouble seeing.[24] Emerging technology could write directly to target neurons that otherwise would get no input at all, essentially creating a (pretty fuzzy) image in the brain based on an artificial eye. But, there's a lot of work between that and replicating healthy natural sight. Cochlear implants also directly contact neurons, and they've been around for decades. But they can only amplify certain sounds, not create a rich and complex auditory scene.

Interestingly, *Fringe* proposed controlling the mind by writing to the thalamus rather than the primary sensory cortex. In "Dream Logic" (2-5), patients being treated for sleep disorders began experiencing terrifying dream states while awake, leading them to attack coworkers and friends whom they believed were monsters or ghouls. Inspecting the body of one of these patients, Dr. Bishop found a brain implant in the thalamus, which he said was the main relay center of all sensory information. This is largely true—all sensory information except smell goes through the thalamus before it goes on to higher processing in the brain. (Unfortunately, Peter commented that the thalamus is a midbrain structure, and his father replied, "Very good, Peter." Sorry, Bishops—it isn't.) When the implant is activated, it stimulates the thalamus in order to provoke the sensory experiences of a dream.

Are the writers on to something here? Is it possible that the thalamus might be the best region to target to produce sensory experiences? It might be, with a lot of caveats. The thalamus

---

24   A. Y. Chow, A. K. Bittner, and M. T. Pardue, "The Artificial Silicon Retina in Retinitis Pigmentosa Patients," *Transactions of the American Ophthalmological Society* 108 (2010).

does not receive the detailed representation of sight, sound, taste, or feeling found elsewhere in the cortex. For example, nearly half the brain is devoted to vision, with specialized regions that process basic lines, shapes, colors, form, movement, and other features. The thalamus, in contrast, is a fairly small structure in the middle of the brain, and very early in the processing chain, meaning that the complex details of sensory perception haven't yet been decoded when they reach it. So, writing to the thalamus could produce some false sensations, but with limited fidelity. There are a few other potential issues, as well. The thalamus is involved in a number of different functions, and tweaking the thalamus could have many side effects. Also, the thalamus is not near the surface of the brain—unlike many of the other cortical regions involved in sensory functions. Therefore, surgery that involves the thalamus is more complicated, expensive, risky, and ethically thorny than sticking some electrodes into the cortex (though, to be fair, the writers of *Fringe* have handled this potential challenge within their plots by establishing that neither Walter nor Massive Dynamic are especially concerned with these four factors). Even if the thalamus did prove to be a useful place to write to the brain, the challenges are such that research into other methods is likely to prove more fruitful, at least for the time being.

Back to Reality

So, are mind reading and mind control possible? Not really—at least not as usually portrayed in bci-fi. It's humbling working with real-world BCI systems, which are generally quite mundane compared with the expectations of many science-fiction fans or (worse) patients and their families.[25] Still, real-world stories have clearly influenced *Fringe*'s writers, and electrode caps off to them for parlaying so much neurotechnology into a popular show. With all of the rapid progress in BCI research, and the increasing attention among so many different people, there are countless emerging opportunities for new bci-fi and neurotechnology plot devices. A front-page story one day might be an episode of *Fringe* the next. It may take somewhat longer for what we see on *Fringe* to translate into new neurotechnology.

⨎ BRENDAN ALLISON earned his PhD in Cognitive Science from UC San Diego in 2003. He has been in BCI research for about fifteen years, working with many of the top researchers and groups. He is currently a Senior Postdoctoral Research Scientist at the Graz University of Technology in Austria.

---

25 J. E. Huggins, "BCIs Based on Signals from Between the Brain and Skull," in *Brain-Computer Interfaces: Revolutionizing Human-Computer Interaction* (New York: Springer, 2010).

F. Nijboer and U. Broermann, "Brain–Computer Interfaces for Communication and Control in Locked-in Patients," in *Brain-Computer Interfaces: Revolutionizing Human-Computer Interaction* (New York: Springer, 2010).

OF WHITE TULIPS AND WORMHOLES

Time Travel in Fringe

STEPHEN CASS

A white tulip from a nonexistent future reveals to Walter Bishop that the Universe is more complex than even he can fathom. In a similar spirit, Stephen Cass shares with us some of the intricacies and complexities of space-time—the fabric of the Universe—and our passage through it.

O ut of thin air, a man appears on a crowded commuter train—and is shaken, but not surprised, to see that everyone else in the car is now dead. He is Alistair Peck, MIT astrophysicist and time traveler. Peck soon finds himself being tracked down by Fringe Division, and the pursuit hinges on the rules and consequences of time travel in the *Fringe* Universe.

Thinking about what the rules and consequences of time travel might be in the real universe has drawn the attention of some of the greatest scientists for over a century. The laws of physics, as we currently understand them, don't seem to forbid time travel, but they're not very clear on how real time travel might work, either. If we could really understand time travel it would mean understanding some of the deepest questions we have about our cosmos and its destiny. What is time? Is everything in the Universe predestined? Why do we feel ourselves existing in the instant of the present, ever moving from the past into the future?

To begin to get a handle on these questions, we're going to have to follow the example of Walter Bishop staring at the equations scribbled all over Peck's apartment . . .

WALTER: If I comprehend this correctly, then this Alistair Peck has taken Einstein's Theory of Relativity and turned it on its ear. I grasp portions of it.

. . . and try to grasp a few portions of Albert Einstein's theories of Special and General Relativity ourselves.

Thinking very deeply about what time is and how we measure it was critical to the creation of Special Relativity. Special Relativity is probably best known for stating the relationship between energy and mass that is the principle behind nuclear reactors and atomic bombs, captured in the famous equation $E=mc^2$. But more importantly for us and Peck, it also established the existence of a four-dimensional *space-time continuum*, where the three dimensions of space are inexorably intertwined with the fourth dimension of time.

Introducing the space-time continuum meant that for the first time, physicists had to consider that time travel wasn't just nonsense dreamt up by science-fiction authors, which must have made H.G. Wells feel a little smug. Wells published his book *The Time Machine* ten years before Einstein published his theory of Special Relativity in 1905. In previous time travel books, such as Mark Twain's *A Connecticut Yankee in King Arthur's Court*, characters were transported by some inscrutable bit of magic, but *The Time Machine* popularized the idea of the deliberate development of time travel technology, grounded in the scientific principles of a four-dimensional Universe.

Still, time travel in Special Relativity is very different from Wells' imagining. In *The Time Machine*, the traveler sits in a contraption that moves into the past and future while remaining in the same spot in space. In Special Relativity, time travel is directionally limited; you can go from the present into the future, but not back into the past. And you can't do it sitting still.

To understand why, let's look at what Special Relativity did to the concept of time. Before Einstein, the notion of *absolute time* was wildly popular in scientific circles, ever since Isaac Newton described it in 1687, alongside a few other clever ideas such as the Three Laws of Motion. Absolute time means that every point in the Universe is ticking along to the same clock. If ten seconds pass in Boston, then exactly ten seconds pass on the surface of Mars, too; time everywhere is in perfect sync, and how objects move through space has no effect on it.

This corresponds to our everyday experience. If you phone a friend, she will report experiencing time at the same rate as you, even if she is on the other side of the country, or traveling in a car (if she is in a different time-zone, her clock will read a different time than yours, but the rate at which the seconds tick by will be the same).

But according to Einstein, the time experienced by an object depends on how it moves through the space-time continuum—in other words, how you move through the three dimensions of space can affect how you move through time. In Special Relativity, objects moving at different velocities relative to each other (hence the name of the theory) have clocks that tick at different rates. Picture one object that's standing still and one object that's zooming through space. From the point of view of the still object (in physics speak, this object is said to be *at rest*), the moving object's clock will appear to be running slow, a phenomenon known as *time dilation*. (It's important to note that from the point of view of the moving object, its clock will appear to be running normally. A second of time will still feel like one second. It's only by comparing the moving and still clocks that the time dilation can be detected.)

The faster the object is moving, the bigger the effect, which is why we don't notice it when talking to friends on the phone—people simply don't normally move fast enough. But imagine an astronaut zooming past the Earth on a spaceship moving at

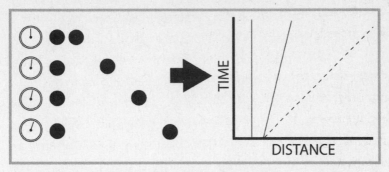

FIGURE 1: On the left is a clock ticking away while one particle stays put and the other particle moves to the right in a straight line. A physicist might chart this motion on a two-dimensional space-time continuum, where the still particle is represented by the vertical line because it moves only in time, not space. The other particle moves in both time and space, so its line is slanted. A particle moving at light speed would follow the dashed line at a forty-five-degree angle. To properly represent general three-dimensional motion, a four-dimensional diagram would be needed.

99.499 percent of the speed of light. For every ten seconds that ticked by for an observer (or Observer!) on the surface of the Earth, the astronaut would only experience one second of time. If the astronaut moved at 99.995 per cent of the speed of light, 100 seconds on Earth would pass for every second experienced by the astronaut. A century on Earth would be just a year of astronaut time. The astronaut would be traveling on a one-way trip into the far future (this is the fate that befell Charlton Heston and his crew in *Planet of the Apes*).

As odd as it sounds, time dilation is not just a theory—it's been measured in particle accelerators. Not for nothing did Peck's old MIT colleague Carol Bryce explain to Peter and Olivia that Peck had been obsessed with particle acceleration. In a particle accelerator, unstable subatomic particles can be boosted to speeds very close to that of light. Normally, at rest, one of these particles might decay in a thousandth of a second, but close to light speed, the measured lifetimes of these particles are increased many times over—time is running more slowly for them, relative to the time experienced by the physicists running the accelerator. Similarly for our astronaut, as she comes closer and closer to light speed, the slower and slower her personal clock ticks from an external perspective, until at light speed, time for her would stop completely. (Remember, time inside the spaceship appears to be moving normally; for her, it's the universe outside that's speeding up as she gets closer to light speed. She would never realize time had stopped, because you need time to perceive and think.)

So, if Special Relativity says we can slow and then stop the clock by going to light speed, could we start it running backward by going just a little bit faster than light? The logic is a little hairy, but if we could, then the result would be full-fledged forward-*and*-backward time travel—we could visit the past, not just the future. So, *can* we make an object's clock go backward? Well, *yes*, followed by a big *no*. First the *yes*, and back to Walter looking at Peck's equation-covered apartment. Noted Walter: "Tachyons are depicted here . . . "

FIGURE 2: The particle on the top left is at rest, while the particle on the top right is moving away at close to light speed. Thanks to time dilation, from the point of view of the particle at rest, time for the moving object is running slowly.

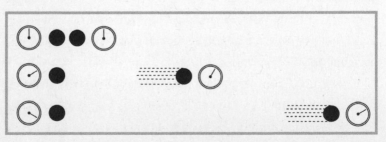

Physicists call the hypothetical particles that travel faster than light *tachyons* (meaning "swift ones"), and it's true that any such particle would be able to travel back in time. But, for now at least, they are entirely theoretical. If they actually exist, these particles must be very different from the kinds of particles that make up you and me, which brings us to the big *no* for using Special Relativity for time travel into the past.

All the protons, electrons, and neutrons that make up the atoms of our bodies have one thing in common—they all have mass. It takes energy to increase the velocity of a particle with mass, and the bigger the mass of the particle, the more energy is required. Right here is where Special Relativity's $E=mc^2$ (which states that energy is equivalent to mass, and mass is equivalent to energy) comes in to bite us in the rear. Making an object go faster— accelerating it so it's traveling, say, one extra mile per hour— increases its kinetic energy. And, because $E=mc^2$, that increase in energy means that now the particle's *mass* has been increased, too. So, in order to accelerate the object by the same amount a second time, you need more energy than you did the first time, because now the particle is just that little bit more massive.

The mass/energy effect is minute and unnoticeable at everyday speeds, but it becomes painfully apparent as you get close to the speed of light—in fact, reaching light speed would require an infinite amount of energy, because the particle's mass would effectively become infinite, too. (Photons, which are particles of light, can travel as fast as they do because they don't have any mass of their own.)

Like time dilation, this increased-mass effect has been veri- fied experimentally in particle accelerators and is the reason why particle accelerators grew from bench-top devices in the early twentieth century, through room- and then building-sized machines, until finally reaching the scale of the current Big Daddy in the accelerator game: the Large Hadron Collider, or LHC. The LHC straddles the border of France and Switzerland and takes the form of an underground ring seventeen miles around filled with superconducting electromagnets. The LHC is designed to pump huge amounts of electricity into the electromagnets in order to accelerate two streams of protons to 99.999999 percent of light speed and smash them together; at the moment of collision each proton will be 7,460 times heavier than the protons that are currently making up the nuclei of the atoms in your body.

Scientists are interested in accelerating particles to such speeds because collisions at higher and higher energies lead to more and more interesting physics that further reveal the fundamental forces and particles that make up our Universe. Pursuing interesting physics without the need for large amounts of pricey European real estate and a staggering power bill is presumably what first motivated Peck to—as Carol Bryce described it—find ways to accelerate particles without a particle accelerator.

So if Special Relativity forbids going backward in time by making crossing the light speed barrier impossible, are there any other possibilities? Well, proving that scientists like sequels as much as movie studio executives, it turns out that there are other possibilities, buried in Einstein's *Relativity: Part Two*. Properly known as the Theory of General Relativity, the follow-up to Special Relativity was published in 1915. (Today, scientists usually combine both theories under the single banner of the Theory of Relativity.) Where Special Relativity just dealt with the comparatively simple case of objects moving with uniform velocities, General Relativity includes acceleration, allowing the theory to handle more types of motion and incorporate gravity.

It wasn't immediately obvious that General Relativity had opened the door to the possibility of traveling back in time, so it was decades before physicists seriously began to consider the idea. Things really got moving in 1974, when Frank Tipler was studying solutions to Relativistic equations as they pertained to motion around massive, very long, rotating cylinders and realized something weird.

To understand what, let's first take a paragraph and look at how gravity works according to General Relativity. Every object that has mass produces a gravitational field. The more mass an object has, the bigger the gravitational field, which is why gravity on the Earth is six times stronger than the gravity on the surface of the Moon—the Moon is a lot smaller than the Earth. But why does this field produce an attractive force? Einstein showed that the attractive force arises because gravitational fields warp space. Think of an ant marching across a piece of paper. This ant is not the brightest member of the colony and only knows how to march in a straight line. Now, imagine bending or twisting the piece of paper (be careful not to squash the ant!). If you looked at the ant from above and ignored the paper, it would look like the ant was walking along curves or turning corners. But the ant is really still just walking in a straight line—it's the terrain that's curved. Similarly, it's the warping of space that causes things like planets to orbit a star or people walking around on Earth to feel a force pulling them toward the center of the planet. Everyone, and everything, is just trying to move in a straight line through the space-time continuum.

Now back to Tipler's cylinder. Around a rotating object, the warping due to gravity has the effect of constantly twisting space along with the object, like a piece of cloth getting wrapped around the axle of a car, an effect known as *frame dragging*[1]. But remember that space and time are part of a continuum, so warping space affects motion through time as well. Tipler realized that the frame dragging effect would mean that if a spacecraft (I did say *massive* and *very long* cylinder!) flew a certain trajectory around the cylinder, it could go backward in time.

The spacecraft would follow what's known as a *closed timelike curve*, returning to the same point in time and space over and over—just like Peck, who can only return to specific times and places in his own past, looping back to an earlier point in the space-time continuum, whether it be a rush-hour commuter train or a field with a balloon he visited one afternoon.

So now we have the blueprint for a real time machine, right? All we need to do is convince NASA to build us a giant spinning cylinder in space and off we go. Unfortunately, Stephen Hawking shot the Tipler Cylinder down in 1992, proving that the cylinder had to be not just long, but *infinitely* long for the math to work out. But by then other physicists had been inspired to see if General Relativity allowed other methods of time travel.

In fact there have been a slew of proposed Relativistic approaches, which include finding flaws in the universe left over from the Big Bang known as *cosmic strings* (these are different to the subatomic strings that feature in String Theory). These very long cosmic

---

1 Notching up another win for the Theory of Relativity, experimental confirmation of the existence of frame dragging was announced in 2011 by NASA's Gravity Probe B mission, which used a satellite to measure the warping of space due to the Earth's rotation.

strings would be incredibly dense and consequently would greatly warp space. In theory, if two such cosmic strings passed close to each other, a spacecraft could fly along a closed timelike curve around both strings to travel back in time. But perhaps the most potentially practical approach is that of Kip Thorne, who, along with some colleagues in 1988, published a paper showing how a *wormhole* could be turned into a time machine.

Thorne's work is why, when Carol Bryce said that the goal of Peck's particle acceleration research was to create wormholes, Peter immediately guessed that Peck's work was related to time travel. Later, Walter illustrated the basic wormhole idea using a piece of paper with a line drawn on it, marked with two times, 10 A.M. and 11 A.M.: he bent the paper over so that the timeline looped back on itself and the 10 and 11 A.M. points coincided. But notice that there was still a problem—in the two-dimensional world of the surface of the paper, the two points were not yet connected by the

FIGURE 3: Walter's paper. 10 A.M. and 11 A.M. are marked at two points on the space-time continuum. When the continuum is folded, the two points are brought close together. A wormhole might be used to travel between the two times.

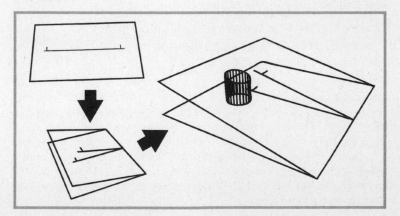

folding—once Walter released his hand the two points would fly apart. If you want to move from the 11 A.M. point to the 10 A.M. point, you first have to find a way to fuse, or build a stable bridge between, these two spots of the space-time continuum, creating a closed timelike curve.

That's just what a wormhole is—it's a shortcut, a bridge between two points in the space-time continuum that would otherwise be far apart. Wormholes are typically thought about in terms of joining two points that are physically very distant (for example, as seen in the *Stargate* movie), but Thorne showed how they could be used to connect points that are far apart in time rather than space (a dodge occasionally employed in the *Stargate* TV spin-offs).

This is how it would work: assuming you somehow managed to create a wormhole in the first place (a short one, for convenience), you then take one of the ends of the wormhole—you can move the end of a wormhole around by pulling it along with an electrical or gravitational field—and accelerate it to near light speed.[2] Time dilation will slow down the rate of time at the moving end. If you can't travel fast enough, General Relativity says you can also use gravity to produce the required dilation—gravitational fields cause time to slow down.[3] So by dangling the

---

2 Moving the end of the wormhole won't change the length of the wormhole itself, nor will the other end be pulled along. Weird, huh?

3 In General Relativity, just sitting in a gravitational field is enough to produce a time dilation effect. And the stronger the gravity, the more time is slowed, relative to someone sitting in a weaker gravitational field. This means that although you may not have realized it, the chances are that you've used a time dilation machine to shift your personal clock. These machines are better known as airplanes—because they fly an appreciable distance above the Earth's surface, where the gravity is just a teeny bit weaker, time moves a smidgeon faster onboard an airplane than on the ground below, albeit by a matter of nanoseconds. This was verified experimentally in 1971 using ultraprecise atomic clocks.

end of the wormhole in a high gravitational field, such as around a black hole, you would cause time to run more slowly at that end. Pull the end out of the gravitational field (or return it from its high-speed trip through outer space), and any time dilation effect will stop. Time will resume ticking at the same rate at both ends of the wormhole.

But because one end spent a chunk of time with its clock running slow relative to the other end, you've introduced a permanent time difference between one end and the other. Say, that using time dilation, you establish a one-hour time difference between the two ends of the wormhole, which you put in opposite ends of the same room. You turn up at 11 A.M., go through the end that wasn't subjected to time dilation, and pop out on the other side of the room at 10 A.M.

So all we need to do is create a wormhole, right? Usually, such a construction project is imagined as being the province of super civilizations, like the aliens that send the instructions for building a wormhole machine in the book and movie *Contact*. But in a few years, depending on whether or not certain theories turn out to be right, human beings could be creating wormholes at the LHC—microscopic ones, but wormholes nonetheless. In these theories, the energy of the collisions could be enough to warp tiny pieces of the time-space continuum, so much so that they are twisted into the shape of a wormhole. But the big problem with wormholes is keeping them open.[4]

Any normal wormhole, of the sort that might be created by

---

4 When scientists first started considering wormholes in General Relativity another big problem was size: initially it was thought that there was a fundamental constraint that limited wormholes to microscopic diameters, but later analysis eliminated this constraint.

the LHC, would be so unstable that it would collapse the moment a single particle entered it—there wouldn't be enough time for the particle to make even a one-way journey. But Thorne and colleagues have proposed that the wormhole could be stabilized and become a *traversable wormhole*.

For this trick, Thorne turned to quantum mechanics, invoking something known as the *Casimir effect*. Quantum mechanics tells us that there's no such thing as perfectly empty space.[5] Instead, even the emptiest void in deep space is a foaming mass of subatomic particles and waves, popping in and out of existence. We don't normally notice these *virtual particles* all around us because they only exist for a very short period of time, but there is a way to feel their presence. Two metal plates placed a millimeter or so apart will exclude long wavelength virtual electromagnetic fields. So, on either side of the plates you have long and short wavelength electromagnetic virtual fields, while inside the plate you just have short wavelength virtual fields. The result of this imbalance creates a small but measurable pressure that pushes the plates together. Thorne and his colleagues believe that this same technique might be used to stabilize a wormhole: the quantum low pressure produced by the Casimir effect could act to pull open the mouth of the wormhole, preventing it from collapsing.

In the laboratory, flat metal plates are used to demonstrate the Casimir effect. But to stabilize a wormhole, you'd need to

---

5 Specifically, the Heisenberg Uncertainty Principle, which places a fundamental limit on how precisely we can measure certain physical properties. In a nutshell, declaring a specific patch of space to be absolutely empty at a specific instant in time would require a very precise measurement of exactly zero for the energy of that space (remember, energy and mass are equivalent thanks to $E=mc^2$), which is forbidden by the Uncertainty Principle.

enclose the entrance in three dimensions. Many times in fiction, the entrance of a wormhole is depicted as a two-dimensional portal that people step through, but an actual wormhole entrance would be a three-dimensional volume of space: a sphere instead of a circle. This, perhaps, is why Peck implanted a conductive mesh underneath his skin. Walter identifies that as a "Faraday Mesh," but what he was talking about is more often called a *Faraday cage*. They take their name from their inventor, nineteenth century British physicist Michael Faraday, who made key early discoveries about electricity and magnetism. Faraday cages are containers made of a conducting solid or mesh, usually metal: an electromagnetic wave can't penetrate the mesh if the holes are a good bit smaller than its wavelength. They're often used to shield electronics from either producing or receiving electromagnetic interference, as when the alternate Brandon demands a Faraday cage be built before turning on the Doomsday machine in the episode "6:02 A.M. E.S.T." (3-20).

Nearly all of us have a Faraday cage in our homes, in the form of the metal mesh in the door window of a microwave oven. Microwaves and visible light are both electromagnetic waves, but the microwaves used in an oven have wavelengths close to five inches long, while visible light has wavelengths measured in a few hundreds of thousandths of an inch. So visible light passes through the sixteenth-of-an-inch holes in the oven door mesh, but the microwaves are blocked.

A Faraday cage would block virtual electromagnetic radiation, too. Perhaps Peck was using the mesh to stabilize the entrance to a wormhole he was opening within himself, expanding the volume of the opening until his body could fit inside the entrance and he could then move through the wormhole to the past.

(That Peck did not have to cover his head and hands in mesh we can attribute to either artistic license or some details of wormhole physics that he alone was privy to.)

But what would happen if you really *could* go back in time? It could lead to all kinds of problems, under the broad heading of *causality violation*. Let's go back to our room, with its one-hour wormhole time machine. You go through at 11 A.M. and emerge at 10 A.M. What if you chose to hang around for an hour after going through the wormhole? Just before 11 A.M. you'd see the earlier you come into the room and get ready to step through the wormhole. What if you stopped yourself from going through? If you stopped yourself going though at 11 A.M., then how did you get back to 10 A.M. to wait around for yourself? In other words, how can you have an effect (arriving at 10 A.M.) if you eliminate the cause (going through the wormhole)? This specific problem is known as the *grandfather paradox*, typically told as the story of a time traveler who goes back in time and shoots her grandfather before he has any children, thus preventing the birth of the time traveler.

Stephen Hawking figured that causality violation would cause such difficulties with the basic operation of the Universe that in 1992 he proposed the *Chronology Protection Conjecture*. This conjecture states that the laws of the Universe, known and unknown, must fit together in a way that makes time travel impossible. Just like faster-than-light travel, or Tipler's cylinder, every time travel strategy that gets dreamt up will prove to have some fatal flaw upon closer examination.

Other scientists believe that causality violation can be avoided if time travel instead follows a rule known as the *Novikov self-consistency principle*, developed by Igor Novikov in the 1970s. This states that the laws of the Universe don't forbid time travel, they just forbid paradoxes. If you arrive at the one-hour time machine to find yourself waiting for yourself, then it is guaranteed that you will go through the wormhole on time. Any effort to stop you made by the later version of yourself will inevitably be doomed to failure: If you try to shoot yourself with a gun, you'll miss, or the bullet will be a dud. If you try to physically block yourself from going into the wormhole you might trip and fall, or have a heart attack; you can no more stop yourself going through than you can walk to the Moon.

At first glance, the Novikov self-consistency principle may seem to be saying that even if time travel is possible, it's impossible to alter the past in any way. Wouldn't any change, however small, cause ripples that would eventually produce a paradox?

But there may be many ways the past could be altered and still produce the same present, at least from the point of view of the time traveler. Imagine in the one-hour time machine room you keep a box. At 9 A.M., a robot puts a set of blocks into the box in some pattern—a cross, say. The box has the feature that the pattern of the blocks can be changed just once, before the pattern is locked. If you come in at 11 A.M. and see the cross pattern before you go through the time machine, then it's guaranteed that whatever you do at 10 A.M., you won't change the pattern. That part of the past is fixed. But now let's imagine the box has a lid, so when you come in at 11 A.M., you can't see the pattern. Now when you go back to 10 A.M., you're free to change the pattern and alter that part of the past or not—either way, what you saw before you entered the time machine (the closed box lid) is the same, and so both possibilities are consistent with the Novikov principle.

This is what the Walter of 2026 is trying to explain to Peter in the third-season finale, "The Day We Died" (3-22):

WALTER: I know the pieces [of the Doomsday machine] were buried millions of years ago, but how did they get there? So deep in the past. But now I understand. I sent them there. The wormhole in Central Park. I sent them back through time. Peter, you can stop the destruction before it occurs.

PETER: If that's the case just don't send the machine back. Then we'll never discover it and I'll never destroy the other universe.

WALTER: No. It doesn't work that way. I have already done it. Therefore, I have no choice but to do it again.

PETER: Walter, that doesn't make any sense.

WALTER: It does. It's a paradox. I can't change what happens because it's already happened, but you can make a different choice within what happened.

What Walter means is that by 2011, he believes that the Fringe Division has done the equivalent of seeing a part of the pattern of blocks from the one-hour time machine example above. That part of the pattern—discovering pieces of a machine that had been sent back through time—is now fixed, not least because it's implied that Walter needs the machine to send Peter's consciousness from 2026 back to 2011. If someone did stop the machine from being sent back, it wouldn't be available for Walter and Peter to use to warn 2011. Stopping the machine from going back could also create a new timeline starting 250 million years ago, the era that the wormhole in Central Park opens to. This would probably make 2011 unrecognizable, depending on how much impact the machine has had in the *Fringe* backstory (remember, the Sam Weisses have been around for generations!).

For 2011 as we know it to exist, the machine must go back. Once Peter goes back in time, though, everything else since 2011 is up for grabs. It's true that this would mean that the people of 2026 would have their timeline replaced by a new history, but even if they knew about it, I doubt the 2026ers would object—their world is about to end, after all. Just so long as someone in some future sends the machine pieces back in time, history will remain consistent with the existence of the 2011 Fringe Division.

The Novikov principle is at the heart of another type of real-world time machine, one that doesn't rely on using Relativity to twist the space-time continuum into knots. It relies on quantum mechanics, and, appropriately enough, was proposed by a real-life MIT professor, Seth Lloyd, late in 2010.

MIT was a good choice for Peck's home institution (and I'm not just saying that because as an editor for *Technology Review*, I'm also an MIT employee!). Scientists at MIT have worked on the issues of time travel for decades, and even the students here are pretty time travel savvy: in 2005, they organized a Time Traveler's Convention, publishing the time and location in as many places as possible in the hopes that time travelers from the future would come across them and journey back in time to the convention. Sadly, no travelers arrived—or if they did, they stayed incognito.[6]

Lloyd's time machine relies on the way quantum mechanics describes things like particles. In quantum mechanics, each particle is associated with a *wave function*. The wave function gives the probability of a particle being located at a particular point in space when you measure its location. Imagine calling

---

6 Just in case some future time traveler is reading this, here are the space-time coordinates: 42:21:36.025°N, 71:05:16.332°W, 08 May 2005 02:00:00 UTC.

someone on their cell phone to find out where they are—they might have an 80 percent probability of being at their desk, a 10 percent chance of being in a meeting, a 5 percent chance of being in the elevator, and so on, but you won't know exactly where they are until you call. Now here's where it gets weird—for something like a person, regardless of whether or not you call them to find out where they are, they are always still in some *one* specific location. But according to quantum mechanics, before you look to see where a particle is, it is, in a sense, in *all* the places it could be, simultaneously. It's only when you make a measurement that a single location for the particle is selected, with the probability of the location given by the wave function (taking a measurement is known as *collapsing* the wave function). Once you've stopped observing the particle, a new wave function emerges. Just exactly how wave functions collapse is still the topic of a great deal of research and speculation. But it is established, through experiments, that it's possible to use wave functions of multiple particles to reinforce or cancel each other out, enhancing or eliminating the possibility of finding particles at a particular spot. It's even possible to make a single particle's wave function interfere with itself in this manner.[7] More weirdness: before it is collapsed, the tail ends of a wave function that describes a single particle never quite fade away to nothing, infinitesimally extending off toward infinity, at least until you try to observe it. This means that there's always a tiny chance that a particle could suddenly appear a long

---

7   This is the reason why electrons in atoms can't just have any old amount of energy, but are only found to exist with specific levels of energy that vary according to which element the atom belongs to—an electron outside one of those energy levels would have a wave function that destructively interfered with itself. All of chemistry relies on this fact.

way away from where it's supposed to be when you do try to observe it, a process known as *quantum tunneling*.

Lloyd and his colleagues reasoned that if the wave function effectively smears the existence of a particle across space, maybe it smears it in time, too. If particles can tunnel through space, why not time? We don't normally detect, say, a particle in an accelerator appearing before the collision that created it, because most of time-tunneling events would violate the Novikov principle in some way and the wave function would get cancelled out. But Lloyd realized how the Novikov principle might be used to create the ultimate computer, capable of performing computations instantly—in essence, he set up a (theoretical) system where all the wrong answers to a problem become the equivalent of grandfather-murdering time travelers and their wave functions get cancelled out. The right answer is the equivalent of the time traveler who spares his grandfather and therefore has a wave function that can go back in time without being cancelled out. By seeing which wave function survives its quantum tunneling to the past, the answer is revealed.

But Peck doesn't seem to follow either Hawking's or Novikov's rules. He's built a machine that allows him to traverse closed timelike curves, breaking the Chronology Protection Conjecture, and then he creates a grandfather paradox, when he chooses to die with his fiancée rather than trying to change time to save her life.

This implies a view of time that's similar to what's described by Brandon in the episode "August" (2-8):

> **BRANDON:** We think of time as linear, right? Life is a journey. You're born, and then you die. And to get from one end to the other, there's only one way through.

[Brandon demonstrates by holding up a tube that's open at both ends and pouring water through it.] Unless you look at it like this. [Brandon refills the tube with water and then traps the liquid inside the tube with his fingers.] Then, you can see any point. It's all happening at once.

In this view, every instant of our Universe's existence, from the Big Bang to the big crunch, or heat death, or whatever other fate may be in store for the cosmos, exists simultaneously with every other moment, like frames coexisting along a strip of movie film (or, for younger readers, like a video file sitting on a hard disk). Our consciousness is like playing that movie film or video file: we see time passing from moment to moment, but the past doesn't cease to exist, and the future already exists—we just haven't gotten to it yet.

This may sound like saying that, like a movie, the past and the present must therefore be fixed. But not necessarily. To see why, a few years ago I created a little computer simulation to explore the grandfather paradox. This simulation creates a very simple and short-lived artificial universe. In this universe, a particle is set up to go through a time machine, return to the past, annihilate the earlier version of itself, and continue on its way. The simulation displays the entire history of the artificial universe as a series of panels, like a comic book, calculating what the entire state of the universe should be at each moment before moving on to the next[8]. So how does the simulation handle the grandfather paradox?

---

8 I put this program together when was I editing *Discover* magazine's science-fiction blog. If you want to see images from the simulation, visit http://blogs.discovermagazine.com/sciencenotfiction/2008/08/04/simulating-the-grand-father-paradox/.

When the simulation is started, the particle goes toward the time machine unimpeded, and then vanishes once it reaches the time machine. The universe continues on into the future without the particle. Once the simulation has finished calculating the entire history of the universe, it goes back to the beginning and starts again. Again, the particle begins to move toward the time machine, but this time, its future self emerges from the machine and "kills" the earlier version of the particle. The simulation runs through the rest of the history of the universe with the future version of the particle going its own way. But the *next* time the simulation begins running through the history of the universe, everything returns to the way things were during the simulation's first run, where the particle *doesn't* meet its future self and goes through the machine. The grandfather paradox forces the simulated universe to oscillate back and forth between two possible histories. Note that from *within* the universe, no oscillation appears to be happening—each timeline has a complete history: but an observer from outside the universe can easily see that two histories are swapping back and forth.

My simulation is very basic and has a number of drawbacks— for one, it uses absolute time, dividing the history of the universe into slices according to uniform ticks of a cosmic clock. And Stephen Hawking would consider it utterly ridiculous, because violating the Chronology Protection Conjecture—allowing a time machine—is built right into the simulation's rules. But the point is that this computer simulation hints at a way that the past, present, and future could all exist simultaneously, and yet still be changeable without paradoxes or the Novikov principle.

One could even imagine that in the real Universe and its lack of absolute time, rather than the entire history of the universe being changed instantly at the moment an alteration is made, changes would propagate down the timeline, like a ripple on a river altering the surface of the water, moment by moment. One could even imagine a series of changes, each working their way along the history of the Universe at the speed of time, creating a number of alternate histories that would all coexist along the timeline, like a chain of boats bumping down a stream. Perhaps this is what the Observer September meant when he said to Walter in the episode "The Firefly" (3-10), "Various possible futures are happening simultaneously."

In this picture, each particle (or time traveler) carries with it its own history that's independent of the rest of the Universe. This would be how Peck was able to send Walter a drawing of a white tulip—despite it coming from a future that would no longer happen from the point of view of Fringe Division. The new history Peck created—the one where he died with his wife, and the team never investigated the mysterious deaths of train passengers—overwrote the original timeline, second by second. But all that's important to the laws of physics—and to Walter's search for a sign of forgiveness—is that, once upon a time, that future *did* happen.

꒦ Originally from Ireland and now based in Boston by way of Brooklyn, **STEPHEN CASS** is a senior editor with *Technology Review*, working just across the river from where Fringe Division's headquarters is supposed to be. He has written about space, physics, and technology topics for over ten years for various publications and was the founding editor of *Discover* magazine's Sci-Fi blog *Science Not Fiction*.

MOO

AMY BERNER

I don't want to seem Bossy, and certainly don't wish to make anybody mad, but before we stampede headlong into the next serious topic, allow me to corral your thoughts and herd your attention to Amy Berner's essay. Amy has an important moosage she'd like to ensure doesn't slip pasture attention, one regarding Walter Bishop's brown-eyed lab assistant. Not Astrid, the udder one: Gene the cow! I'd lay steak that you, too, will find her essay udderly delightful.

"The cow is of the bovine ilk; one end is moo, the other, milk."

–OGDEN NASH

"The only thing better than a cow is a human. Unless you
need milk. Then you really need a cow."

–WALTER BISHOP

W alter Bishop—our Universe's version—is a tough nut
to crack. He has no problem experimenting on children. He'll happily push both others and himself past their physical and emotional limits in the name of science. The ends do
tend to justify the means as far as Walter is concerned. But there
is one . . . not person, *entity* perhaps, that he cares for and
protects far more than the people in his life: his trusty lab cow.

Gene the Cow is the SpongeBob Squarepants–loving mascot
of *Fringe*. She was referred to originally as a handy "ethical test
subject," but she has become more of a pet project and raw milk
source for Walter, a one-animal petting zoo for young lab visitors, and an in-joke for the other characters; Peter used the name
"Gene Cowan" while staying off the radar ("Northwest Passage"
2-21). For any character visiting the lab for the first time, she
stands as an instant signpost that Walter's lab is anything but a
standard FBI facility. But even more importantly, with as dark,
twisted, and just plain gross as *Fringe* can get, we—and the characters—need a presence like kind-eyed Gene. For the audience,
Gene is the "spoonful of sugar" that makes the more disturbing

parts of *Fringe* easier to bear. Walter might be digging into the innards of human brains or almost-human spinal columns, but Gene creates a friendly background, lightening a grisly scene simply by hanging out in her well-kept pen. With a well-timed "moo" (listen for them, they happen more often in the background than you might think!) or a lick of greeting, Gene's presence can add to character commentary, create a laugh, or simply break a scene's tension.

But Gene herself begs the question: why have a cow in the lab? True, Walter loves raw milk and strawberry milkshakes, plus having her around to care for and milk must be a nice diversion at times. But what are the roles of *Bovidae Bovinae Bos Taurus* in science? Especially as they relate to current genetic research, because . . . well, duh, her name is Gene.

When Walter requested a cow when making his "must have" list for the lab, he was very specific: "Purebred, not a crossbred, this is important. Mature weight 850 pounds, total fat average 2.37" ("Pilot," 1-1). Miss Gene herself is a standard American dairy farm cow (or possibly a heifer) and most likely a Holstein, a breed that originated in the Netherlands and currently makes up 90 percent of the total of dairy cows in the United States.[1]

But again, why a cow? According to Peter Bishop, "Genetically, cows and humans are distinguishable by only a few lines of DNA. Ethical test subject" ("Pilot"). The *Fringe* pilot aired in September of 2008, almost a year before the cow genome had been fully sequenced. With that new data in mind, is a cow truly all that great of a test subject and a replacement for a human,

---

1   University of Kentucky Department of Agriculture, "The Dairy Industry: Dairy Breeds—Holstein."

genetically-speaking? All living things on Earth (this version, anyway) do share parallel genes, and our fellow mammals share much more DNA-wise with us humans than, say, a cabbage (which is genetically 40 percent similar to a human if you're curious).

Based on the genome mapping research completed in 2009 on Dominette, a Hereford cow in Montana, we're only 80 percent similar to cows.[2] It may sound like a lot, but we're also 60 percent similar to fruit flies and, as Walter informed Astrid in "Reciprocity" (3-11), 50 percent similar to bananas (which is true,[3] by the way). Members of the rodent family have a much higher percentage of similarity and thus are more standard test subjects for the scientific community; rats hit 90 percent similarity. Bonobos (also called pygmy chimpanzees) win at the human-similarity game, coming in at 98 percent.[4] So, when we learned that William Bell had designed a retroviral serum based on Walter's DNA that would regrow his brain tissue, we can understand why Walter craved bananas rather than hay after taking it.

But while we're not all that similar to cattle genetically, we certainly base a huge part of our planetary existence on them. As of 2009, there were 1.3 billion cattle on the planet. The top cow countries are, in order, India (where the slaughter of a cow is forbidden by law in almost all of its states), Brazil, China, and the United States.[5] Speaking of Brazil, guess the source of their

---

2   Randolph E. Schmid, "Cow Genome Unraveled to Improve Meat, Milk" *Associated Press.*

3   "Bananas," Things You Don't Need To Know.

4   Kira Zhaurova, "Genomes of Other Organisms: DNA Barcoding and Metagenomics," *Nature.*

5   Belinda Ary, "Cattle Today" http://cattle-today.com/, and http://faostat.fao.org.

leading cause of greenhouse gas emissions? Cattle farming. It's responsible for four-fifths of the deforestation of the Amazon rainforest and three-fourths of the burning of forests and vegetation throughout the country.[6]

According to the USDA, Americans ate 26.9 billion pounds of beef in 2009. We exported 1.868 billion pounds, and the total value of the cattle industry in the United States was $73 billion. And in a subject near and dear to Walter's dairy-loving heart, we produced 14 billion pounds of cheese and 1.6 billion pounds of butter that year as well.[7] The United States produces more corn than any other country, and 55 percent of that corn goes to feed livestock, including cows. It takes seven pounds of corn to produce one pound of corn-fed beef.[8]

Why is this important? The cow genome wasn't mapped for just scientific curiosity. The main reason it was examined was for a very practical purpose: agriculture. It's a gigantic part of the American economy and, according to the Office of Public Affairs, the second-biggest source of American exports.[9] We devote a huge part of our resources to the cattle industry, and the understanding of the cow genome helps the industry improve production.

Most of Walter's side projects with Gene have been dairy-related (and, unlike some of his experiments on humans, quite

---

6 Mario Osava, "Cattle, the Ignored Predator," Terraviva.

7 United States Department of Agriculture Economic Research Service, "U.S. Beef and Cattle Industry: Background Statistics and Information."

8 United States Department of Agriculture, Economic Research Service, "Corn Prices Near Record High, but What About Food Costs?"

9 United States Department of Commerce International Trade Administration, "U.S. Trade Overview."

humane). He has looked into making chocolate milk from the inside, although an effective substance that Gene could easily and comfortably digest through the four compartments of her stomach has not yet been found. He also considered feeding Gene a serum a fellow scientist had created to prevent cell decay, creating milk and cheese that would never spoil, a huge boon to the dairy industry, but he refused to do so "until [he understood] the long-term side effects" on his cow ("Marionette," 3-9).

In another side project, Walter hooked Gene up to solar panels for unknown reasons; Peter said he was nearly electrocuted by that one. My conjecture regarding why he may have done this is that he was attempting a method of internal pasteurization. Pasteurization is the process of heating a food—or, more often, a beverage such as milk—to a specific temperature for a set length of time, then immediately cooling it down, in order to slow microbial growth and keep it fresh longer. Walter is a big raw (meaning unpasteurized/unhomogenized) milk fan, as evidenced by his attempt to import it home from Ohio, but most states in the United States as well as Canada heavily regulate it. Proponents of raw milk claim that pasteurization and homogenization destroy or damage some of the milk's nutrients,[10] destroying beneficial bacteria along with the bad ones such as salmonella (though the U.S. government disagrees with this claim[11]). Gene's solar panel outfit may have been part of an attempt on Walter's part to pasteurize the milk without losing the nutrients or bacteria.

---

10 Raw-milk-facts.com.

11 Food and Drug Administration, "Memoranda of Information, M-I-03-4: Sale/Consumption of Raw Milk-Position Statement."

Science has made advancements in another area of bovine research for the purposes of agricultural advancement: cloning. As it happens, three similar Holsteins have played our trusty bovine to date: one in the pilot, one in season one, and one starting at the start of season two, each brought in when the production moved to a different city (Toronto, New York City, and Vancouver, respectively). As far as we know, these cows all came into being the standard way, but cloned cows have become increasingly common in the United States and Canada in the last decade.

Cloning has long been a part of modern agriculture; in fact, every banana that most Americans have ever eaten is a clone (not only are bananas incredibly difficult to breed conventionally, they are also highly susceptible to disease if not altered to resist).[12] Cloned livestock, however, came onto the scene more recently and has caused much more controversy. Since Dolly the sheep became the first cloned mammal in 1996 (but not revealed until 1997), scientists have pursued cloning of other types of livestock, including cows. The very first cloned calf was born on February 7, 1997, in Deforest, Wisconsin, and named, appropriately, "Gene." That Gene lived a full life at the Minnesota Zoo Education Center.[13] Another first came in 2000, when a Japanese cloned cow gave birth to a healthy non-cloned calf.[14] The University of Georgia created a procedure in 2001 that led to increased success in bovine cloning. Then, in 2003, Canadian scientists created the first Holstein clone, creating "Starbuck II" from a

---

12 Dan Koeppel, *Banana, The Fate of the Fruit that Changed the World.*

13 Minnesota Zoo, "Cow."

14 BBC News, "Cow Clone Gives Birth."

frozen cell harvested from "Starbuck," a premiere bull who had died five years earlier[15] (insert *Battlestar Galactica* joke here). In January 2008, the U.S. Food and Drug Administration declared milk and meat from cloned animals safe for human consumption, allowing cloned food products to freely enter the American food supply from that point forward. The United States' National Cattlemen's Beef Association also supports cow cloning.[16]

Europe has tougher regulations on cloned animals in agriculture; European law states that all foodstuffs produced from cloned livestock must pass a safety evaluation and gain authorization before they are marketed to the public. However, in 2010, a few unauthorized cows sneaked through and became dinner for unwitting consumers. The resulting investigations discovered that up to a hundred descendants of one cow clone now live in Great Britain.[17]

Is that all Gene and her fellow cows, bulls, calves, and heifers are good for, then? Various forms of human consumption, like steaks and sticks of butter and pairs of boots? Not at all. For example, meet Iowa's Bessie the Cow. In 2001, Bessie gave birth to an adorable calf named Noah. Baby Noah, however, was not your standard bovine. He was a gaur, a type of endangered ox that is native to Asia. Scientists used a cow's egg cell and replaced it with the nucleus of a gaur skin cell in order to create the baby ox. Bessie was actually not the first cow to give birth to a gaur. Before Bessie, other cows had carried "test-tube" gaurs to term, but Bessie was the first to truly mother a cloned gaur. Unfortunately, little Noah

---

15   Ron Ravelley, Sounds Like Canada, "Canada Enters the Clone Age."

16   National Cattlemen's Beef Association, "Cloning."

17   DiscoveryNews, "Cloned Cow Meat Enters Food Chain."

died due to an infection a few days later, but Bessie's success showed that such a thing was possible.

Cows have also become a key to cloning other animals, including *homo sapiens*. This area of cloning is referred to as "therapeutic cloning," also known as somatic cell nuclear transfer. This concept may bring up images of bodies grown for their organs—or perhaps humans wandering around mooing—but that's not the case. Cows, or rather, their eggs, are being used to develop processes to manufacture human stem cells, and this research has been going on for quite some time. In 1999, British scientists revealed that they had created the first hybrid human embryo months prior. It was November of 1998 when the scientists successfully combined a cell from a man's leg and a cow's egg. The first hybrid embryo developed for twelve days before it was destroyed.[18] This procedure is still in development throughout the world toward the possible production of viable human stem cells, but the research is not currently federally funded in the United States.

Why use a cow egg? Wouldn't a human egg work just as well? Yes, but human eggs are in short supply and require surgery, while cow's eggs are much easier to come by. A 2006 BBC report explains the process:

> They would insert human DNA into a cow's egg which has had its genetic material removed, and then create an embryo by the same technique that produced Dolly the Sheep. The resulting embryo would be 99.9% human; the only bovine element would be DNA outside the nucleus of the cell. It

---

18   BBC News, "Details of Hybrid Clone Revealed."

would, though, technically be a chimera—a mixing of two distinct species into one. [19]

I know what you're thinking. But no, children have not resulted from these experiments. If William Bell's DNA is floating around somewhere in Massive Dynamic (and really, how could it not be?), Walter can't grow a new version of him quite yet, with or without Gene's help. Fifteen states have laws pertaining to human cloning, the first of which was California's ban on human reproductive cloning in 1997. Human cloning became illegal in Massachusetts in 2005, so Walter's lab is covered as well. However, there are no federal laws in place at this time; government agencies follow the official policies of the federal government in regards to cloning instead.

The official U.S. government stance on human cloning, via the U.S. Department of Energy Office of Science, Office of Biological and Environmental Research, Human Genome Program, is twofold. First, it would be dangerous and inefficient because of the low rate of success in other mammals, both in the percentage of live births and health issues that lead to a high mortality rate. Second:

In addition, scientists do not know how cloning could impact mental development. While factors such as intellect and mood may not be as important for a cow or a mouse, they are crucial for the development of healthy humans. With so many unknowns concerning reproductive cloning, the attempt to

---

19   Fergus Walsh, "Plan to Create Human-Cow Embryos," BBC News.

clone humans at this time is considered potentially dangerous and ethically irresponsible.[20]

"Human Cloning Prohibition Acts" have been introduced in the 105th, 107th, 108th, 109th 110th, and 111th Congresses, including three in 2007 alone, two in the House of Representatives, and one in the Senate. Most did not make it out of committee. The two that did passed the House but never made it to the Senate floor. In statements regarding restoring federal funding to therapeutic cloning, President Obama had this to say about human reproductive cloning in 2009: "We cannot ever tolerate misuse or abuse. And we will ensure that our government never opens the door to the use of cloning for human reproduction. It is dangerous, profoundly wrong, and has no place in our society, or any society."[21]

But back to cows. As I looked into various Interesting Cow Facts, my research took a sudden left turn into quantum mechanics (because, with *Fringe*, one does that sort of thing). I stumbled across the 1975 "COW Experiment." This particular experiment had nothing to do with bovines; COW stands for the scientists R. Colella, A.W. Overhauser, and S.A. Werner. And what were they studying in this particular experiment? "Parallel particles." Coincidence? We are talking about *Fringe*. For all we know, there's a parallel version of Gene whose position in its universe has changed her as well, just as the genetically identical

---

20 U.S. Department of Energy and National Institutes of Health, U.S. Human Genome Project, "Cloning Fact Sheet."

21 Fox News, March 9, 2009.

Olivia/Fauxlivia (or Bolivia, if you prefer) and Walter/Walternate have both been affected by their environments.

However, as far as we've seen, there's only one Gene . . . and her plush stall environment is unlikely to be found in the red universe. Walter has treated her as a pet, as a hobby, and as an occasional unwitting accomplice rather than as a standard research subject. Otherwise, Walter milks her, brushes her (or has Astrid do it; downward strokes only, of course), walks her, brushes her teeth, introduces her to lab guests, gives her Chinese food to eat, and protects her from the horrific sight of Peter eating cheeseburgers. And while he unreservedly experiments on himself, on Olivia, and, as referred to in "In Which We Meet Mr. Jones" (1-7), even on his own (sort of) son when he was a boy, to Walter, Gene appears to be as off-limits when it comes to dangerous experiments as human children are to Walternate. For now, anyway.

AMY BERNER is an event planner by day, but she's also obsessed with television and pop culture and she loves to write about both. She's appeared in nine Smart Pop anthologies so far, including *Five Seasons of Angel, The Anthology at the End of the Universe, Alias Assumed, Farscape Forever, Neptune Noir, Getting Lost, In the Hunt,* and *Filled with Glee.* She also cowrote *The Great Snape Debate* with Orson Scott Card and Joyce Millman for BenBella Books/Borders Press. She lives in San Diego and never misses Comic-Con.

WALTERED STATES

NICK MAMATAS

At first blush 1960s icons Timothy Leary and G. Gordon Liddy couldn't be more different, yet their lives were inexorably intertwined. Although not "bipolar" in the colloquial sense of the term, clearly Walter Bishop circa the early 1980s had within him the seeds to become either, as modern-day Walter and Walternate demonstrate. One theme at the core of *Fringe* is that our actions have repercussions—sometimes extreme ones. Nick Mamatas explores aspects of these two polar opposite personalities—both in our world and the life of Walter Bishop—as well as the events and repercussions that can unlock the Liddy or Leary within.

One Pill Makes You Smaller . . .

Walter Bishop is one of the most beloved television characters in recent memory. In addition to getting all the best lines on the program, and thanks to John Noble's scenery-chewing performances, Bishop was one reason to give *Fringe* repeated chances during its shaky first season. But there are plenty of genius kooks on TV; what makes Bishop stand out is his uncomplicated use of psychedelic drugs. Even Dr. House eventually suffered the consequences of his Vicodin abuse and went straight (at least temporarily), but Bishop actually gains insights into the super-scientific conundrums he faces thanks to drug use. And now, thanks to a glimpse into the other universe, we know what Bishop would look like without a constant supply of psychedelics (and with all the parts of his brain intact): the cold and authoritarian Walternate.

The Walter/Walternate conflict seemed doomed to destroy the two universes. Yet, these geniuses are the only people mentally capable of saving both their worlds. In a September 2010 interview, John Noble hinted that the two characters he plays may yet come to an accord. "What's got to happen is that there has to be peace made," he told E! Online. "If this breach is indestructible, what if the two great minds of each world got together and said, 'We know how to fix it.'"[1] Can it happen? The season-three finale suggested that Walter and Walternate may yet join forces.

---

1 Megan Masters, "Gasp! Is *Fringe*'s Walternate Actually a Good Guy? John Noble Sure Thinks So," E! Online.

There's a real-world duo—one who captured the essence of the conflict between the drug-fueled counterculture on the one hand, and law and order on the other—who might be able to shed some light on this question: Timothy Leary and G. Gordon Liddy. Both were great seekers in the 1960s, but what they sought and how they used their intellects were quite different. Leary explored inner space through LSD and other methods of altering consciousness, and with the insights so gained looked to re-create the world as a freer place. For Leary, altering perceptions was the tool with which he transformed society—just like Walter. Liddy was also interested in changing society and also used perception to do it. But rather than beginning by altering his *own* perceptions, Liddy was a great believer in creating spectacles and manufacturing threats. He used his intellect and cunning to convince the world of a great danger in order to perpetuate his own power. That is, G. Gordon Liddy is none other than Walternate.

First There Is a Walter, Then There Is No Walter, Then There Is

The radical politics and metaphysics of the 1960s and the authoritarian backlash against them are explicit themes of *Fringe*. Series cocreator Roberto Orci even referenced Ted Kaczynski—the genius mathematician who enrolled at Harvard at age sixteen and later became the terrorist Unabomber—in creating the character of Walter Bishop. The so-called ZFT (*Zerstörung durch Fortschritte der Technologie* or "Destruction by advances in technology") manifesto, for example, was based on "the kinds of things that were going on at Harvard where the character of

Walter Bishop studied in the sixties and seventies . . . what if we made it seem as if Walter had written the Unabomber's manifesto?"[2] Executive producer Jeff Pinkner adds that the "notion of questioning reality, and questioning constructs, and questioning authority . . . is this the only reality" heavily informs the show and specifically the character of Walter Bishop.[3]

One can't help but read the above and think of Timothy Leary. There are many commonalities between the pair. Both were born in Massachusetts—Bishop in Cambridge and Leary in Springfield. The Boston metro area is known as the Athens of America, and for good reason. There are dozens of colleges and universities in the area, and young people come to Boston from all over the world to study there. Precocious locals often never leave—it's not at all unusual for a bright young man or woman to treat Harvard, MIT, or one of the other elite universities a bus ride from their home as their local "safety school." *Fringe*, minus the usual failures of continuity inevitable in TV, captures the spirit of the Boston area very well, and this spirit is reflected in Bishop's character . . . and Leary's real life.

Both Bishop and Leary were scholastic achievers, with Walter Bishop attending Harvard as an undergraduate and the real-life Leary enrolling in West Point on the eve of the Second World War. Perhaps not surprisingly, Leary didn't mesh well with the military academy's rigorous demands—he was "shunned" by his fellow cadets and received demerits for the most minute infractions of the rules. Eventually, he returned home to a local college

---

2 See "The Sixties and Themes of *Fringe*," The Paley Center for Media (video interview).

3 Ibid.

as well: Holy Cross in Worcester. Bishop completed his PhD at MIT before getting a job across town back at Harvard, the same local school where Leary ended up as a professor.

Walter and Leary even met once! As Walter reminisced during "A New Day in the Old Town" (2-1), *Fringe*'s second-season opener:

> **WALTER:** This is an experiment that Belly and I did. We came up with such a spectacular blend of drugs. One day, Leary came by, and he said, "You're kidding me."
>
> **ASTRID:** Is this gonna make her head explode or something?
>
> **WALTER:** Well, in a sense, yes, but not physically. We're trying to augment her fifth, sixth, and seventh chakras.
>
> **ASTRID:** Throat, third eye, and crown.
>
> **WALTER:** That is correct, Asterix.
>
> **ASTRID:** Astrid.
>
> **WALTER:** Communication, speech, clairaudience, cognition, and thought. Spirituality.

This scenelet is interesting because it not only connects Bishop and Leary physically—they both apparently worked at Harvard at the same time—but also philosophically. That even Leary was wary of Walter and William Bell's experiment is notable because of Leary's reputation for breaking the rules of science by experimenting on himself, and on others. Declared "the most dangerous man in America" at one point, social guru Leary declared that the youth of the 1960s should "tune in, turn on, and drop out" of the empty and authoritarian society of the immediate postwar era—with the help of lysergic acid, or LSD.

But Leary wasn't just some trippy-hippy dude. He was a fairly renowned psychologist and the director of psychological research at the Kaiser Foundation Hospital in Oakland, California, before returning home to Massachusetts to accept an appointment at Harvard. Only after Leary's Harvard Psilocybin Project (in which he administered psychedelics to professors and intellectuals) and Concord Prison Experiment (which supposedly reduced recidivism rates significantly) landed the psychologist in hot water with Harvard[4] did he move on to mysticism. His 1964 book, *The Psychedelic Experience*, is typical of his work post-Harvard, in that it is as multidisciplinary as Walter Bishop's. Science and mysticism combine in Walter's experiments, just as they do in Leary passages such as this one: "One allows the energies to travel upwards through several ganglionic centers (*chakras*) to the brain, where they are sensed as a burning sensation in the top of the cranium."[5] It's a tribute to Leary's influence that, forty-five years after his book was published, the word "chakra" can be used *sans* tedious exposition on broadcast television.

Walter, too, is a visionary; the changes he makes in himself allow him to perceive the world differently and then work to change it. As Special Agent-in-Charge Phillip Broyles famously said, the Fringe Division's cases are "as if someone conducting experiments, but with the whole *world* as a *lab*" ("Pilot," 1-1)—and the world is Walter's lab, just as his own body is a testing ground.

---

4 Harvard president Nathan M. Pusey went on record claiming that Leary was let go because he didn't show up for his classes.

5 Timothy Leary, Ralph Metzner, and Richard Alpert, *The Psychedelic Experience: A Manual Based on the Tibetan Book of the Dead.*

Indeed, what makes Walter a Leary analogue is how he pursues knowledge. Fringe science is so named not only for its wild inquiries and spectacular results, but for its fringe practices. Walter experimented, heavily, on himself, as well as on those around him. In addition to his constant tinkering with drugs, he, with the help of William Bell, removed parts of his own brain. When Massive Dynamic recovered serums supposedly designed to regenerate that grey matter, Walter didn't wait for testing to determine whether the serums—the labels to which had been lost—would work; he ingested one immediately and ended up having an adventure with a brain full of chimpanzee DNA.

For Walter, the personal experiments and their results are what inform his attempts to change the world. Walter was a failure though; his mind was shattered, his experiments soured, and his naïveté ultimately served to the entire planet. There are many who would suggest that the social upheavals of the 1960s have done the same to the minds of many participants and also serve to threaten our future.

Leary's search for universal knowledge also began with the self. He was on a personal "trip" that lasted his entire adult life, and that trip was also a social one. He began looking for a new way to live, not just for himself but for all humanity. His mansion home in Millbrook, New York, wasn't just a party house, but a way for Leary to fund his research—"[G]uests would pay sixty dollars to sit and meditate in the many empty rooms of the house."[6] Leary also moved beyond LSD; he investigated many other ways of altering consciousness and experimented on the

---

6 Don Lattin, *The Harvard Psychedelic Club: How Timothy Leary, Ram Dass, Huston Smith, and Andrew Weil Killed the Fifties and Ushered in a New Age for America.*

guests. Some ways of altering consciousness were weirder than others—Leary liked to serve eggs and milk dyed green and black for breakfast, just to challenge the sensory expectations and experiences of his guests. Of course, Walter is constantly experimenting with snack foods, sometimes with similar results.

Leary's most audacious plans match Walter's in scope. In the 1970s, Leary announced what he called his S.M.I^2.L.E.[7] project—that's Space Migration, Intelligence Increase, Life Extension. It's proper fringe science and involved the sort of social engineering Walter and William Bell would be putting into practice in the 1970s of the *Fringe* universe. Leary envisioned a colony ship of hundreds of fertile and intelligent people leaving the Earth and claimed that the human personality itself was evolving to create new temperaments and personality types ready for the rigors of space travel and near-immortality. Walter, with his hard science background, went beyond prediction and started actually directing evolution with his nootropic drug cortexiphan. The healthiest beneficiary of the treatment, Olivia, has in fact tuned in, turned on, and . . . become an FBI agent. Well, two out of three isn't bad.

Leary's S.M.I^2.L.E. project also hints at other elements of *Fringe*'s themes and overarching plot. He claimed to be the recipient of "transmissions" by alien intelligences. One of the transmissions explained, "Life was seeded on your planet billions of years ago by nucleotide templates which contained the blueprint for gradual evolution through a sequence of biomechanical

---

7 Often just called SMILE, this concept was first articulated in Leary's book *Exo-Psychology: A Manual on The Use of the Nervous System According to the Instructions of the Manufacturers.*

stages."[8] These beings, with their long-term plans for us, clearly have something in common with the "First People" of *Fringe*, who may have built the weapon capable of destroying whole universes (or who may have sent them back in time, from the future, as Walter suggests in "The Day We Died" [3-22]), or who may be leading humanity toward a better tomorrow.

Then there is Leary's connection with a variety of countercultural groups, which is reflected in Bishop's relationship with ZFT, the secret society of techno-terrorists funded by William Bell. Leary even used his scientific acumen to escape from prison. When sentenced, he was reportedly given a personality test—the Leary Interpersonal Behavior Test, an instrument of his own design. Having perfect knowledge of the answers, he manipulated his responses to the test and landed an assignment as a gardener under minimal security. He promptly escaped and was transported to Algeria with the help of the radical left terror group the Weather Underground—another obvious inspiration for ZFT. Leary's connection to radical groups kept him out of the hands of the state—and on the run in Algeria, Switzerland, Afghanistan, and elsewhere—for a few years. Leary finally reentered prison in 1973 (right around the time G. Gordon Liddy did).

Finally, there's the Nixon connection. Nixon was the one who labeled Leary "the most dangerous man in America," and the feeling was mutual. In the third-season episode "Concentrate and Ask Again" (3-12), Walter revealed that he, too, had a Nixon encounter. "Tricky Dicky" he said, wanted to turn one of his and William Bell's experiments into a weapon; Walter quickly quit

---

8   Quoted in Richard Metzger, *Book of Lies: The Disinformation Guide to Magick and the Occult*.

and abandoned the line of research, though ultimately the bone-melting technology was weaponized without Walter's help.

Will

Timothy Leary is most famous for what he ingested, as is lawman turned ex-convict G. Gordon Liddy. But whereas Leary consumed LSD, Liddy consumed . . . a rat. As a test of his will-power and to conquer his fear of rats, he roasted a dead rat, skinned it with a knife, and ate its haunches. Liddy was eleven years old.

Liddy studied law, joined the FBI, and later became a prose-cutor for Duchess County, New York, the location of Leary's Millbrook mansion. Liddy was not about to stand for the famous radical running a bizarre drug den under the guise of science in a nice suburban neighborhood and decided to take action. According to author Jay Stevens in *Storming Heaven: LSD and the American Dream,* "Leary, sequestered behind the stone portals of the Hitchcock Estate, reminded Liddy of Dr. Franken-stein." Liddy also saw the opportunity for a media spectacle; if he could capture Leary and "expose" him, Liddy's political career would be made. The bust had all the making of a daring commando raid, and also of a sex farce. Liddy and his crew waited for the lights to go out, but were concerned with a blue flickering light emanating from the windows. At first, they decided that the Millbrook guests were watching a pornographic film, but soon discovered that they were in fact watching a looping film of a waterfall. (Probably while high.) Finally, Liddy kicked down the door and was greeted by spontaneously written folk songs and a pantsless Leary, who insisted that one day a statue of himself would be erected on the site.

Liddy made his bones with his bust of Leary just as he had planned and quickly found his way into the employ of President Richard Nixon. There, Liddy became a "plumber" whose mission was to deal with the embarrassing press leaks that Nixon believed were harming his presidency. Despite his law-and-order conservatism, Liddy had a flair for the audacious. One of his plans to ruin the campaign of Democratic presidential hopeful George McGovern, for example, involved recruiting hippies to enter McGovern's hotel suite during a press conference and then arranging for, as he put it in his autobiography a *Will*, "every dirty hippie there [to] whip it out and take a leak, right there in front of everybody."[9] He also plotted to drug Daniel Ellsberg, the military analyst who released the Pentagon Papers to the *New York Times*, with LSD with the assistance of "Cuban waiters."[10] Then there was the mysterious break-in at the Watergate, orchestrated by Liddy for reasons that are still mysterious—Liddy's own story about compromising photos was likely just a red herring. He was sentenced to twenty years in prison on charges of conspiracy, burglary, and illegal wiretapping but served only four-and-a-half years for the crimes, thanks to a commutation of his sentence by President Jimmy Carter and subsequent parole.

Liddy and Walternate are much alike. They use their knowledge of the world and its levers of power to remake the world in the image of their own aspirations and their own nightmares.

---

9   The plan was vetoed by U.S. attorney general John Mitchell, who had booked the suite for immediately after McGovern's departure.

10   Liddy, *Will: The Autobiography of G. Gordon Liddy*.

Liddy was perhaps the first prominent example of the vision of history and human agency described in this famous quote from one of then-president George W. Bush's aides in 2004:

> The aide said that guys like me were "in what we call the reality-based community," which he defined as people who "believe that solutions emerge from your judicious study of discernible reality" . . . "That's not the way the world really works anymore," he continued . . . "when we act, we create our own reality. And while you're studying that reality—judiciously, as you will—we'll act again, creating other new realities . . . We're history's actors . . . and you, all of you, will be left to just study what we do."[11]

Liddy was not a member of the reality-based community; he was a member of the reality-rewriting community. He saw the world as he knew it as under attack from outside forces, ones that often literally identified themselves as "far out." And when those forces didn't exist, he worked to create them. Liddy remade the American system nearly as completely as Walternate has in *Fringe*, in his role as the architect of what has come to be called the War on Drugs. As Edward Jay Epstein noted in *Agency of Fear: Opiates and Political Power in America*, "Liddy foresaw the full potential of the drug issue as an instrument for reorganizing agencies of the government . . . Because they were dealing with an unprecedented 'epidemic,' any innovative measure, no matter how unorthodox, could be considered and discussed."

---

11   Ron Suskind, "Faith, Certainty and the Presidency of George W. Bush," the *New York Times Magazine*.

It began with Operation Intercept, a Liddy brainchild, on the Mexican border. On September 21, 1969, every vehicle crossing the border between Mexico and the United States was stopped and searched for illegal drugs, with minimal input from or warning to the government of Mexico. Relatively few drugs were seized, but that was hardly the point of the three-week exercise. The Republicans could now claim to be tough on drugs in a time when casual drug use was seen as the key to enlightenment, and as Liddy himself put it, "Operation Intercept, with its massive economic and social disruption, could be sustained far longer by the United States than by Mexico. It was an exercise in international extortion, pure, simple, and effective, designed to bend Mexico to our will."[12]

Having put on a show of saving middle America from the terrors of Mexican marijuana, Liddy soon turned his eye to the Middle East, and heroin was elevated to a national security issue. The War on Drugs was on, and forty years later it continues to this day. Indeed, since the law enforcement crackdown on illegal drugs was not actually designed to be effective—but rather designed to grant law enforcement ever-greater powers of surveillance, arrest, and seizure—the war *must* continue.

Thanks to the War on Drugs, the United States now has the second-highest rate of incarceration in the world. One million Americans are incarcerated every year on drug law violations. Foreign policy is heavily influenced by the War on Drugs as well. The United States invaded Panama in 1989 with 25,000 troops in order to arrest former CIA asset and Panamanian leader General

---

12 Liddy, *Will.*

Manuel Noriega.[13] U.S. intervention in Afghanistan is also part of the drug war—though hundreds of millions have been spent to eliminate the heroin poppy fields in that country, the end result has thus far been years of record harvests and farmers whose fields have been wiped out siding with and funding the Taliban in its war against American forces.[14]

The similarities between Liddy's reality-altering and Walternate's are clear. Putatively, Walternate is devoted to law and order— Walter refused to build weapons for Nixon, but Walternate built the "Star Wars" antimissile shield for Ronald Reagan. (It's also telling that Walter consumes psychedelics and Walternate drowns his sorrows in the most bourgeois of depressants: booze!) The "other" America, under Walernate's direction, is virtually a police state with mandatory identification cards—the "Show Me"— necessary even to use public transportation. Nixon never resigned in disgrace; indeed, his image is on the silver dollar. Ten thousand people, trapped in "amber" quarantine thanks to tears in the universe for a decade, have been declared legally dead, and enormous swaths of the country, including most of the Boston metroplex, are uninhabitable. The FBI, a civilian law enforcement agency, has been disbanded and the Fringe Division has been rolled into the Department of Defense, making it essentially a military division. The environment is a mess, Nevada appears to be independent entirely of the United States, and smallpox continues to infect human beings. There are substantial technological advances in the

---

13 In a twist suitable for prime-time television, George H. W. Bush was the head of the CIA when Noriega was being funded by that organization, and president when Noriega was deposed.

14 Armen Keteyian, "Inside The Afghan Poppy Wars: Is The U.S.-Led War On Drugs In Afghanistan Undermining The War On Terror?" CBS News.com.

parallel universe, of course, including easy travel to the Moon and workable nanotechnological medicine—is this what we could have expected had the Walter of "our" Universe not been in the mental hospital for decades? That is, if Walter was not the casualty of his own Learyesque mind-expanding trips?

Walternate, like Liddy, needed a *bête noire* for his own ambitions, and like Liddy Walternate decided that Walter and the entire counter*universe* (never mind counterculture!) would fit the bill. Walternate sees his world as on the verge of collapse to the influence of a whole other way of being, and Walter as the kidnapper and despoiler of children. This matches exactly the conservative view of the 1960s—the old order was falling to ruin, thanks partially to reprobates like Leary and his influence on the youth. It's no coincidence that after Leary's death in 1996 both the *New York Times* and *Los Angeles Times* declared him the "Pied Piper" of a generation in their obituaries.

Walternate's response to this self-created threat is also much like Liddy's—he has militarized his world and cemented his own power, but has also engaged in a number of weird and inexplicable antics. The incidents that make up The Pattern—the leaking of military coordinates to a coma patient; the destruction of an airline flight thanks to a passenger's monstrous transformation; the disappearance of children and their reappearance years later without having aged—are Walternate's doing,[15] but speak more to his individual audacity and his willpower than anything else. These events are his version of trying to dose Daniel Ellsberg with LSD—fight fire with fire!

---

15 While it's never been explicitly stated that Walternate caused these events, it has been heavily implied. And really, who the hell else could it be?

And then Walternate lost. His universe was destroyed, and by his own hand. This drove him entirely outside the law—not only is there no longer a United States for him to represent as an official, the entire world he helped create has been destroyed. The irony is delicious, and not dissimilar from Liddy's own adventures. Liddy always presented himself as a law-and-order type, and yet not only did he manipulate the laws in order to cause a crisis he could solve, he ended up breaking the law, without ever changing his opinion of himself.

The Best of Both Worlds?

John Noble has suggested that ultimately Walter and Walternate must work together to heal the rifts between their worlds. Leary and Liddy ultimately joined forces as well: in 1982, sixteen years after Leary was arrested by ·then–district attorney Liddy, the two actually became friends and staged a series of debates on college campuses. Their reasons for teaming up, however, had less to do with saving two universes than saving two bank accounts. Their debate was a rehearsed back-and-forth, complete with rejoinders and jokes. Liddy claimed that the counterculture had led to an America that had fallen into chaos, while Leary insisted that despite the victory of the counterculture, America's political parties were essentially Mafia families and that repression and authoritarianism could return to the United States at any moment. Of course, it can be persuasively argued that both Liddy and Leary are correct—they are describing our Universe, which is as messed up in its own way as Walternate's is.

In 1996, as Leary neared death from prostate cancer, Liddy

said of Leary, "[He was] wrong . . . but he thought he was right, and he was trying to do good as he saw it."[16] An intriguing claim from the old ex-felon, one that demonstrates a glimmer of insight and integrity. And it is perhaps no coincidence that it matches almost exactly John Noble's comment on Walternate, one of the two mad geniuses he plays on *Fringe.* "Walternate is a good man," Noble told E! "He's saving his world. If our world was disintegrating, we'd want someone to step up; that's truly what Walternate does." Walternate failed to step up, but the events at the end of season three have given him a chance to save "our" Universe, and to reclaim his own, with Walter's help. Indeed, to truly save any world—even ours—we need the knowledge that comes from a clear perception of the world unhampered by the status quo and society's taboos, and the knowledge borne of the will to reorder reality itself. We need both Liddy and Leary, both Walter and Walternate.

✯ **NICK MAMATAS** is the author of several novels, including *Sensation* (PM Press) and with Brian Keene, *The Damned Highway* (Dark Horse). His writings on culture and politics have appeared in the *Village Voice, H+, The New Humanist, In These Times,* and many other venues. As an editor of short fiction, anthologies, and now Japanese science fiction and fantasy in translation, Nick has been nominated for Hugo, World Fantasy, Bram Stoker, and Shirley Jackson awards.

---

16 Pamela Kramer, "Setting Stage for Final Trip: Cryonics, Cyberspace in Counter-Culture Guru's Plans for Demise," Knight-Ridder Tribune News Wire.

FRINGE DOUBLE-BLINDED ME WITH SCIENCE

ROBERT T. JESCHONEK

From the first-season episodes (not as disordered or disconnected as perhaps first they seemed) to a starring character whose
antics, not long ago, would have been censored right off prime-time TV,
to on-screen messages encoded in cryptic glyphs, the series *Fringe*
itself seems like an experiment in fringe television. Up next, Robert
Jeschonek reports his own experimental findings on *Fringe*.

Has any dramatic TV series ever been as experimental as *Fringe*, in the sense that its subject matter focuses on literal experimentation?

Fringe deals more with scientific experimentation than any regular series since *Watch Mr. Wizard*. Almost every episode deals with experimentation and its consequences. Typically, the stories revolve around experimental subjects run amuck, empowered by some extreme fringe-science treatment. Rogue scientists continuously push the limits, conducting trials that generate one menace after another, whether technological (the killer video of "No-Brainer" [1-12]), animal-derived (the multi-species hybrid creature of "Unleashed" [1-16]), or something that twists the physical laws of the Universe (the vortices opening up between parallel universes, as seen in multiple episodes including "6B" [3-14]). The Fringe Division team—Walter, Olivia, and Peter—must find a way to stop the menace, usually through new and ever more outrageous experiments.

Hypothesis 1: Human Trials Can Cause Side Effects

One of the most frequently employed types of experiment featured in *Fringe* can also be seen as the most ethically compromised: the unsanctioned human trial.

In our world, in the United States at least, research involving human subjects is strictly controlled. As a rule, we don't hear much about unauthorized human experimentation; if it happens, it doesn't often make the headlines. In the world of *Fringe*, however, unsanctioned human trials and their consequences are undeniably widespread and a matter of great interest. Again and again, Olivia, Peter, and Walter encounter the results of experimental treatments administered to human beings: the man who disrupted electricity ("Power Hungry," 1-5); the woman who became a spinal fluid vampire ("Midnight," 1-18); the genetically altered baby who survived death to become a superhuman cannibal ("Night of Desirable Objects," 2-2); the people turned into human bombs by a military experiment ("Fracture," 2-3). In each case, treatments that have presumably passed through other experimental stages—theory, bench testing, animal testing—are moved to the next level and applied to humans.

However, the rogue scientists confronted by Fringe Division aren't the only ones who have performed hazardous human trials. Walter, the very genius who helps take down the rogue researchers week after week, has also been responsible for the same brand of human experimentation. In fact, plenty of the threats encountered by the Fringe team arise from past human trials conducted by Walter and William Bell.

Many *Fringe* episodes focus on Walter and his team working to undo his own legacy of dark deeds involving human subjects. For example, Walter's work thirty years ago to develop a fast-growing soldier fueled a deadly project to keep a rapidly aging man alive by feeding him the pituitary glands of murdered women ("The Same Old Story," 1-2). During another project for the military, Walter injected a man with an organo-iridium compound, turning him into a receiver for secret radio messages from a ghost network; years later, the signals drove the test subject mad, though Walter managed to intercept the signals and help thwart a terrorist attack ("The Ghost Network," 1-3). In yet another case, Walter's work to develop camouflage techniques using electromagnetic pulses to scramble the human optic nerve made it possible for a town of deformed individuals to conceal their true nature from unsuspecting visitors ("Johari Window," 2-12).

The highest profile human trials in *Fringe*, by far, are the cortexiphan trials, in which Walter and Bell administered a perception-enhancing nootropic drug to young children in Florida and Ohio. According to Walter, "William theorized that it might enhance certain abilities in predisposed children" ("Bad Dreams," 1-17).

Decades after the cortexiphan trials, subjects developed extraordinary powers, often with catastrophic results. For example, subject Nick Lane became a reverse-empath, able to influence people's emotions ("Bad Dreams," 1-17). He caused a woman to kill herself by jumping in front of a subway train; he also caused a woman to stab her husband to death in a restaurant. Another cortexiphan subject, James Heath, developed the ability to heal himself by transferring illness to other cortexiphan subjects ("Olivia. In the Lab. With the Revolver," 2-17). Before his capture by the Fringe team, he killed multiple victims by infecting them with rapid-onset cancers.

The most notable cortexiphan trial subject, in terms of *Fringe*'s mythology, is of course Olivia Dunham of Fringe Division. During the original cortexiphan study, when she was a child, a cortexiphan-related reaction caused her to experience a pyro kinetic event ("Subject 13," 3-15). She developed the ability to see an aura (or "glimmer") around people and things from a parallel universe, which she retains as an adult. And her cortexiphan-altered physiology also allows her to move back and forth between the prime universe and the parallel one.

Hypothesis 2: Ethics Arise from Abuses

Olivia's cortexiphan-spawned abilities have proven invaluable during the cold war with the parallel universe . . . but the question remains: how ethical were the human trials in the first place? The children enrolled in the study were too young to understand the dangers involved or provide any kind of informed consent. Never mind that cortexiphan promised tremendous benefits to humanity and theoretically would only be effective when administered to children. The lack of informed consent still signifies an ethical deficit in the case of this study.

Past trials in the United States have also lacked informed consent and so been seen as unethical. One of the most infamous cases was the Tuskegee syphilis experiment, in which the U.S. Public Health Service studied the progress of untreated syphilis in 399 African-American sharecroppers in Tuskegee, Alabama. During the study, which ran from 1932 to 1972, the sharecroppers were never told they had syphilis, or that it could be treated effectively with available antibiotics.[1] Numerous study participants died of syphilis or related complications; participants' spouses were infected, and babies were born with congenital syphilis.[2]

---

1 "U.S. Public Health Service Syphilis Study at Tuskegee," www.cdc.gov.

2 "Remembering Tuskegee," www.npr.org.

In a related study in the late 1940s, U.S. researchers deliberately infected 696 Guatemalan prison inmates, women, and mental patients with syphilis, then treated them with penicillin to test the drug's effectiveness. Dr. John C. Cutler, a Public Health Service physician who later worked on the Tuskegee study, ran this syphilis program in Guatemala.[3]

As a result of public outcry over experiments like these, the Office for Human Research Protections (OHRP) was established. Whenever human subjects are involved in experimentation funded by the Department of Health and Human Services, the research must be approved in advance by OHRP and monitored by Institutional Review Boards (IRBs) regulated by the agency.[4]

In the world of *Fringe*, however, rogue scientists don't worry about things like informed consent, OHRP, or IRBs. Human experimentation by underground researchers waits for no regulatory agency that might slow the development of fear-inducing hallucinogens ("The Dreamscape," 1-9), giant killer slugs grown from the common cold virus ("Bound," 1-11), mind-control drugs ("Of Human Action," 2-7), or huge parasitic worms that infest and kill human hosts ("Snakehead," 2-9). Bleeding-edge scientific giants like Walter haven't paid much attention to regulations in years gone by, either. Did he and Bell go by the book while developing a delivery system for involuntary mass inoculation in the 1970s, a system that might have been the prototype for a deadly bioweapon ("Concentrate and Ask Again," 3-12)?

---

3 Maggie Fox, "U.S. Apologizes for Syphilis Experiment in Guatemala," www.reuters.com.

4 *Code of Federal Regulations Title 45, Public Welfare, Department of Health and Human Services, and Title 46, Protection of Human Subjects,* www.hhs.gov.

Did Walter seek IRB approval when he gave Rebecca Kibner treatments, including LSD, that enabled her to see shape-shifters ("Momentum Deferred," 2-4)? It doesn't seem likely. Walter's current situation, however, is very different, as his human subject-based field work is sanctioned by the FBI. Federal approval of his extreme methods, seen as necessary to deal with extreme circumstances, seems to be implicit.

But if Walter and Bell existed in our reality and received federal funding for their human research from any agency of the Department of Health and Human Services, they would have to follow strict regulations. Walter and Bell would have to work with OHRP to obtain a Federal-Wide Assurance, an agreement acknowledging that they will adhere to all federal laws and regulations related to human subjects research. In addition, Walter and Bell would have to obtain approval of their experimental design from an IRB specifically designated by OHRP as overseeing the research in question. The process of obtaining IRB approval can take many months, depending on the nature of the proposed study and the backlog of other cases being handled by the IRB at the same time. It can be a difficult process with unexpected hurdles and delays along the way, but it does help to prevent the abuse of human subjects in experimental trials.

Hypothesis 3: You Are a Lab Rat

The real-world system of regulation represented by OHRP only prevents a certain kind of human experimentation, however. Other human trials are exempt from federal rules and happen all around us all the time.

For example, we are all subjected to informal social experimentation every day as part of our interactions with other people. Our fellow human beings constantly form hypotheses about what we might do or say under certain circumstances. Then, they test those hypotheses by subjecting us to variables and watching our reactions. The results of these experiments confirm or disprove their hypotheses and shape their future behavior toward us.

Then there are the trials that are less individualized and more likely to have a widespread impact: large-scale product testing conducted regularly in the consumer marketplace, which amounts to a de facto nationwide human trial.

If the Food and Drug Administration (FDA) deems a product fit, after appropriate testing and human trials, for consumption by the public, the manufacturer is free to market it. At this point, a much larger de facto human trial takes place as consumers use the product, and the manufacturer tests a new hypothesis: that the results of the initial trials will extend to the entire population of future users.

When a new food, drug, medical device, or other FDA-regulated product reaches a nationwide cohort of users, its effects can be unpredictable, in spite of previous results among limited population samples. By using a new product, we help substantiate earlier findings of its lack of harmful effects . . . or disprove those findings by suffering a negative impact.

History has shown that products that make it to market, even after testing and trials, can still be far from harmless. Thalidomide, for example, was widely used outside the United States in the late 1950s and early 1960s as a remedy for insomnia, morning sickness, and other maladies. Hailed as a "wonder drug," thalidomide turned out to have horrific side effects, causing deformities in thousands of children of mothers who'd used it in forty-six countries.[5]

More recently, the anti-acne drug isotretinoin, sold in the United States under the name Accutane, was subjected to stricter controls after users reported side effects including depression, alopecia (hair loss), inflammatory bowel disease, degenerative disk disease, bone disease, and rosacea.[6] Birth defects were also an issue, as with thalidomide.[7] This was another case in which a drug made it through tests and trials, then triggered negative outcomes when it reached a broader cohort of test subjects in the general population.

By serving as participants in de facto human trials in the consumer marketplace, we act as human lab rats. But the characters in *Fringe* are lab rats in yet another way: they are subjected to a myriad of experiences in the course of daily life that could be unrecognized experiments performed by unknown—perhaps unknowable—entities.

Hypothesis 4: The World Is One Big Petri Dish

When Olivia first uncovered a clue to the activities of ZFT, a group responsible for secretive scientific research, Homeland

---

5   Linda Bren, "Frances Oldham Kelsey: FDA Medical Reviewer Leaves Her Mark on History," FDA *Consumer Magazine*, www.fda.gov.

6   "Isotretinoin," *Wikipedia*.

7   Anick Bérard, Laurent Azoulay, Gideon Koren, Lucie Blais, Sylvie Perreault, & Driss Oraichi, "Isotretinoin, Pregnancies, Abortions and Birth Defects: A Population-Based Perspective," *British Journal of Clinical Pharmacology*.

Security Special Agent Phillip Broyles, head of Fringe Division, told her the group might be responsible for certain parts of The Pattern.

> **BROYLES:** What we've learned so far is the following: there are cells—we don't know how many. Privately funded with presence in eighty-three recorded countries. ZFT is among them.
>
> **OLIVIA:** So they're terrorists.
>
> **BROYLES:** Not in the conventional sense. They traffic not in drugs or weapons, but in scientific progress.
>
> **OLIVIA:** Meaning what?
>
> **BROYLES:** Meaning what happened on Flight Six-Two-Seven, or what happened to Agent Loeb. These may have been simply proof that a scientific theory, an experiment—worked.

A key theme of *Fringe* is that the world is one big petri dish, a laboratory in which a multitude of overlapping, interlocking experiments are ongoing. In fact, Broyles once described The Pattern, the series of weird science-driven events investigated by the Division, "as if someone out there is experimenting, only the whole world is a lab" ("Pilot," 1-1). Broyles offered his description in the first episode of *Fringe*, and it only became more fitting as time passed.

In *Fringe*, there is a constant stream of experimentation under way, and usually, the person performing an experiment is revealed quickly. Their motives are also uncovered, which helps humanize these unorthodox experimenters, whether they are villains-of-the-week (like Dr. Robert Swift and Cameron

Deglmann, who created a hybrid creature ["Unleashed," 1-16]) or Walter and Bell. The cortexiphan trials, for example, were initiated by Walter and Bell in the prime Universe to develop superhuman defenders to fight off an invasion from the parallel universe. Conversely, "Walternate" in the parallel universe performs experiments to activate Olivia's reality-crossing powers and mount the very invasion feared by Walter and Bell. Later, he builds a machine to destroy Walter's Universe. His motive? To save his own universe, which has been unraveling since Walter abducted his son, Peter.

But we aren't *always* shown the rationale behind the experiments and events depicted in *Fringe*. We don't always know who is performing these experiments, or why. Sometimes, unanswered questions linger, suggesting mysterious influences at work. For example, when a strange metal cylinder emitting a unique audio frequency emerged from underground, it became the subject of a deadly search. By the time it burrowed back into the Earth, the Fringe team still knew next to nothing about it, only that a man dubbed "the Observer" wanted to ensure it returned safely below ground ("The Arrival," 1-4).

The Observer himself, named "September," represents another unexplained phenomenon. Hairless, otherworldly, unable to enjoy food unless it's doused in flavoring, and equipped with advanced technology, September appears at the scene of every major Pattern-related event. He rescued Walter and young Peter when they first crossed over from the parallel universe ("Peter," 2-16), and he escorted Walter to his old beach house to prompt him to find the device that could plug holes between the prime Universe and the parallel one ("There's More Than One of Everything," 1-20). He is one of a group of men who look, dress, and act alike—all hairless,

business-suited, and exhibiting strange mannerisms. During the
course of the show, we meet at least four of them: September,
August, December, and July. (I say at *least* four, because we also
met a child character with certain Observer traits who might be a
juvenile form of these beings ["Inner Child," 1-15].)

September's true nature and motives are known only to him
and the other Observers. Is he helping conduct secret experiments in the prime and parallel worlds of *Fringe*? At one point,
he did admit to experimenting on Walter. During a series of
events revolving around Walter's rock legend hero, Roscoe Joyce,
September asked Walter to do something that could lead to
Peter's death. Walter trusted September and did what he asked
("When the time comes, give him the keys and save the girl."),
which, to his relief, did not end Peter's life. While meeting with
a fellow Observer named December later that episode, September
said, "I must admit, I feared my experiment would fail."

> **DECEMBER:** But you were right. He's changed. He was
> willing to let his son die.
>
> **SEPTEMBER:** Yes. And now we know. When the time
> comes . . . he will be willing to do it again. ("The Firefly,"
> 3-10)

The Observers' cryptic comments were illuminated later,
when Walternate managed to activate the Universe-damaging
machine built from parts and designs attributed to "The First
People." As the prime Universe began to rupture, Walter realized the only way to save it would be to let Peter enter the
version of the machine that existed on their side of the dimen-
sional wall. As much as Walter loved Peter, he risked losing him

to save the Universe, a sacrifice predicted by his actions in the Roscoe Joyce affair in "The Firefly." The outcome: Peter punched a hole between the two universes, providing a stable zone in which their denizens could meet to try to stave off a catastrophic end . . . and then he disappeared. Not only did Walter and Olivia lose him, they lost all *memory* of him as well.

As Peter vanished, at least ten Observers gathered outside the stable zone on Ellis Island, noting the implications of this event:

> **DECEMBER:** You were right. They don't remember Peter.
>
> **SEPTEMBER:** How could they? He never existed. He served his purpose. ("The Day We Died," 3-22)

These comments suggest the Observers have indeed been conducting an experiment designed to yield this expected outcome. It seems logical to assume that all the events they've manipulated during their interventions were intended to lead to this. So maybe the Observers do see the two universes as their own personal petri dish. Perhaps their goal from the start has been to merge the two universes, or prove that two dependent and highly complex systems can coexist in some kind of steady state . . . or simply to demonstrate that cooperation can win out over conflict, even in an end-of-the-world scenario where the chief participants are flawed and selfish human beings. Whatever their hoped-for endgame, the Observers seem to show little in the way of concern for the emotional impact of the events they guide and monitor. They note Peter's nonexistence as a simple fact, with no regard for how it affects those who care about him.

The Observers personify what some might say is the scientific ideal: the scientist as an unemotional, perfectly objective entity, dedicated only to experimentation for the advancement of knowledge. For the most part, the Observers uphold this ideal, reacting without emotion and expressing interest only in performing their mysterious experiments.

But how much does the Observers' objectivity help to ensure the validity of their experiments? How much does *any* researcher's objectivity matter during the completion of a study? Ultimately, observation itself provides a demonstrable impact on any experiment, regardless of the objectivity of the observer.

Hypothesis 5: The Observer Affects the Observed

According to a phenomenon known as the Observer Effect (which surely must have been on the *Fringe* writers' minds when they came up with the Observers featured in the series), the act of observation brings about changes in the physical properties of a thing being observed. Inevitably, the equipment or techniques used to observe the state of a thing alters that very state, skewing the results from what they might be if no observation had been needed to acquire them.[8]

For example, an electron can only be detected if a photon interacts with it. But when that happens, the path of the electron is changed. Thus, the measurement of the electron's position is not really accurate, because the very act of viewing it has caused it to change position.

---

8 "Observer Effect (physics)," *Wikipedia*.

Another example can be found in temperature measurement. To determine the temperature of a substance—hot water, for example—you must insert a thermometer into the substance. But the thermometer absorbs some of the thermal energy contained by the substance, which alters the actual temperature being measured, however minutely. The instrument changes the measurement.

This effect is quite evident in *Fringe*, as the Observers affect the people and events they observe. September saved Peter as a boy ("Peter") and later used him to restore the balance disrupted by that very rescue ("The Firefly"). The Observer named August saved the life of a woman destined to die, causing the other Observers to send an assassin whose own death led to her salvation ("August," 2-8). The involvement of the Observers shades the mind-sets of the Fringe team, increasing their drive to seek answers. For example, when Olivia, Walter, and Peter realized a woman's abductor was an Observer, they threw themselves into tracking him down with a great sense of urgency ("August").

This alteration of mood, which in turn alters consciousness and behavior, could be an unintentional influence stemming from the bias and expectations of the Observers themselves. When individuals participating in human subject experimentation know they're being observed, this awareness can cause them to change their behavior. The Subject-Expectancy Effect, for example, occurs when test subjects influence the outcome of an experiment because of their own expectations of the likely or desired outcome.[9] Similarly, the Observer-Expectancy Effect

---

9 "Subject-Expectancy Effect," *Wikipedia*.

occurs when observers influence an experiment's outcome based on their biased expectations.[10] These effects are part of a phenomenon known as reactivity.

Hypothesis 6: Blinding Makes Validity Visible

To ensure the validity of an experiment, researchers must control for reactivity by the implementation of blinding techniques in which information is withheld from experimenters and/or test subjects.[11] In blind or single-blind experiments, test subjects aren't given specific information that could affect their responses; for example, subjects in a drug trial might not be told if they're in the group receiving an experimental drug or the control group receiving a placebo.

In double-blind experiments, neither the test subjects nor the experimenters are in possession of all information. In the example of a double-blind drug trial, neither the subjects nor the experimenters would know which specific subjects are in the control group and which are in the experimental group.[12] This technique increases the likelihood of a scientifically valid outcome with minimal impact from reactivity. The more invisible the experimenter, the more accurate the trial; thus, a single-blind experiment is more accurate than one with no blinding at all, and a double-blind study is more accurate than either of those.

---

10 "Observer-Expectancy Effect," *Wikipedia*.

11 "Reactivity (psychology)," *Wikipedia*.

12 "Double Blind Experiment," Experiment-Resources.com.

It goes to follow that if the Observers of *Fringe* are indeed conducting some kind of experiment involving the two parallel universes, it must be a double-blind one. The inhabitants of the universes certainly seem to have no idea what the Observers are up to. The Observers, on the other hand, possess an almost omniscient awareness of the experimental conditions and possible outcomes . . . but their awareness doesn't allow them to predict everything in perfect detail. For example, September made a mistake when he saved Walter and Peter during their crossing from the alternate reality, and he had to correct it with their help ("The Firefly"). So it seems the Observers are not perfectly omniscient, which supports the possibility that their grand experiment is a double-blind one. They are the gods of a double-blind world, manipulating people and events to prove or disprove a mysterious hypothesis of their devising. Perhaps they already proved this hypothesis when Walter sacrificed Peter to save the two universes ("The Day We Died"), or perhaps the experiment's final results have not been seen yet.

But even with the control afforded by double-blind design, perhaps an unintended effect is also at work. As carefully as the Observers manipulate the experimental controls, variables, and subjects, perhaps the subjects are having an unexpected influence on *them*.

Who's to say reactivity can't extend to the influence of test subjects on observers? Maybe the act of working with human subjects can change an experimenter's approach, expectations, and behavior. Perhaps these changes can then feed back and affect the experiment.

We've already seen examples of altered behavior in *Fringe* Observers. When August saved the life of a doomed woman, the

Observers sent an assassin after him because he had broken the rules ("August"). Why did he save her? August described his reasons thusly:

> **AUGUST:** I saw her many years ago. She was a child. Her parents had just been killed. She was crying. But she . . . she was brave. She crossed my mind . . . somehow. She never left it. I think . . . it's what they call . . . feelings. I think . . . I love her.

As the Observers otherwise never seem to express emotions during their appearances in *Fringe*, this showed that August had clearly been influenced by a subject of his observation. The Observed had changed the Observer. The lab rat had altered the researcher.

And if the lab rat can alter the Observers, how much control do the Observers really have over the experiment? Is it possible that the control they seem to exert over the variables of the experiment is just an illusion? If so, perhaps the characters in *Fringe* have more free will than they know.

Or perhaps someone *else* is pulling *all* of their strings, controlling human and Observer alike.

Hypothesis 7: An Über-Pattern Exists

The Observers might not necessarily represent the top of the experimental food chain in *Fringe*. There could be other forces exerting an influence beyond even them, conducting an even vaster experiment. Perhaps these higher powers are the true gods of the double-blind world, manipulating events to extract results in support of grander hypotheses than the Observers anticipate.

Fringe hints at this possibility. Bell, while inhabiting Olivia's body ("Stowaway," 3-17), discusses fate's impact on the Fringe team's latest adventure:

> **BELL:** Well, destiny, fate. Jung called it synchronicity, the interconnectedness of apparently unrelated events. I mean, don't you think that it's curious we meet a woman who is unable to die at the exact moment my consciousness seemingly returns from the grave? Now as a scientist, I like to believe that nothing just happens, that every event has some meaning. Some sort of message. You just have to be able to listen closely enough to hear it.

Could it be that the meaning and message to which Bell referred are indicators of an über-Pattern implemented by powers beyond the ken of humanity and Observers alike? If so, perhaps it's best to stay true to the mythology of the show and not venture into the metafictional realm; let's assume Bell was not winking at the audience, referring to *Fringe*'s existence as a television series in our own "real" universe. Is it possible that the synchronicity of events in *Fringe* is indeed part of a grand experimental design carried out by a higher intelligence?

If so, where does free will enter the picture, if at all? Each episode of *Fringe* presents us with a series of bizarre events, often born in a laboratory, that trigger mayhem. Walter, Peter, and Olivia must race against time to prevent further mayhem by employing experimental techniques to unearth clues and devise solutions. Along the way, it feels very extemporaneous, as if the characters are moving spontaneously from one step of the investigation to the next, except when the Observers intervene and push them one way or another. But what if the humans and Observers alike are all being guided by experimental conditions directed by upper-level, unseen gods? What if these supreme experimenters possess the overall experimental design identifying whether participants are controls or actual experimental subjects? Does the fate of the prime and parallel universes rest in their hands?

Is this, perhaps, the fundamental theme of *Fringe*, that all reality might be an ever-expanding series of concentric circles, each representing another level of experimenter manipulating variables in the next level down? Or is this tantalizing idea merely a thought experiment that complements a different core message?

Perhaps the driving purpose behind the experimentation of *Fringe* is much simpler and more obvious, but no less thought-provoking and important to our world.

Hypothesis 8: Mad Scientists Are People, Too

Fringe invites us to witness experimentation from all sides and identify with all participants. We sympathize with subjects like Olivia . . . Simon Philips the mind reader ("Concentrate and Ask Again") . . . or the paraplegics enabled to defy gravity ("Os," 3-16). We feel sorry for innocent bystanders who suffer because of rogue experimentation, like the plane crash victims ("Pilot") and the bus riders trapped in amber ("The Ghost Network").

But we also understand the mad scientists who cause so much havoc by plying their trade. We meet men like Dr. Crick ("Os"), who helped paraplegics defy gravity, though he knew it would kill them, because he wanted to cure his paraplegic son. We get to know people like Dr. Penrose ("The Same Old Story"), who directed the murders of women and the removal of their pituitary glands, because he needed them to cure an experimental subject who had become like a son to him.

And, of course, we become extremely well acquainted with Walter Bishop, who jeopardized the very existence of two universes simply because he reached out to rescue a doppel-ganger of his dead son, Peter. Is it possible not to feel sympathy for this redeemed devil as he watches the fabric of his home Universe fray and splinter because of his long-ago experiments in crossing over? The pain of knowing he might be responsible for the end of the world is enough to break his heart, and ours.

Fringe makes us care about, or at least understand, the experimenter as well as the experimental subject and the innocent bystander affected by experimentation. It's a unique approach that increases our understanding of all facets of the experimental process . . . and that's a good thing in a day and age in which experimentation occurs constantly across a wide range of disciplines and shows no signs of slowing down.

When we fail to see research subjects as three-dimensional human beings rather than anonymous factors in an equation, we diminish the very humanity we seek to advance with the tools of science. We end up with atrocities like the Tuskegee syphilis study and the human suffering caused by thalidomide and Accu-tane. Similarly, when we lose sight of the humanity of the scientists conducting experimentation, we risk setting them apart from their subjects, when in reality the wall between experimenter and subject is perilously thin.

It's much easier, if scientists are seen as being different and distant from their subjects, to believe they are somehow beyond human concerns and ethics. It's far better to impose *Fringe*'s view on the architecture of experimentation, in which all participants influence each other profoundly, no matter which end of the microscope they're on.

ROBERT T. JESCHONEK wrote *My Favorite Band Does Not Exist*, a young-adult fantasy novel of alternate realities, time travel, and rock 'n' roll, available from Clarion Books and Houghton Mifflin Harcourt. Robert is an award-winning writer whose fiction, comics, essays, articles, and podcasts have been published around the world. Robert's work has been featured in Smart Pop's *House Unauthorized* and *In the Hunt: Unauthorized Essays on Supernatural* and in publications from DC Comics, Simon & Schuster, and DAW. Visit him online at The Fictioneer website, www.thefictioneer.com, and www.tsetsepress.com. You can also find him on Facebook and follow him as @TheFictioneer on Twitter.

MASSIVE DYNAMIC

Progress and the Science of Destruction

JACOB CLIFTON

In the 1990s, *The X-Files* succeeded in part because it played to our paranoid sense that *someone is doing something somewhere that's going to be bad for us . . . I just know it!* How counterintuitive and frightening is it, then, to have a colossal and well-funded institution of scientific research like Massive Dynamic—the bastion to which we look for the solutions to today's problems—be an enabling force for another entity called Zerstörung durch Fortschritte der Technologie (Destruction through the Advancement of Technology)? Massively dynamic Jacob Clifton investigates for us the fringe science of destruction, damnation, and redemption.

> "You will make all kinds of mistakes; but as long as you are generous and true, and also fierce, you cannot hurt the world or even seriously distress her. The world was meant to be wooed and won by youth."
>
> —WINSTON S. CHURCHILL

The Conspiracy of Unhappiness

In the science community you hear a lot about "pure research," that Grail of exploration in which money is no object and the marketable endpoint—weaponry, biotech, anything that can be bought and sold—is removed from the equation. Of course, scientists and medical researchers are not useful for their daydreaming, and the simple fact of capitalism means pure research is purely fantasy.

Because scientific experimentation requires training, materials, and space to work, funding must come from somewhere: the academic community, the government, big business. All of which come with their strings attached, their red-tape bureaucracy, and all of which frequently cross over into each other a bit more than we might like.

Conspiracy theorists will tell you we are being blocked—from the transhumanist singularity, from curing cancer and AIDS, from saving the oceans and skies—by this profit motive. It is not in the interests of Big Pharma, for example, to cure the diseases they profit from treating. No more sick patients means no more pharmaceutical industry, and then where would we be? Preventative medicine is another pure research goal with no financial means of support: without sick patients, the insurance industry would die on the vine, and then where would we be? They're too big to fail, as we say these days.

Now personally, I think most conspiracy theories have their roots in a sort of civic pathetic fallacy: Since something is happening, somebody must be doing it. Since drugs are killing the inner city, it must be the Republicans or the communists providing cheap addiction. HIV began in certain demographics, and therefore those demographics must have been targeted.

There's a lot to unpack in those theories. A lot of fear; a lot of love, in the strength of our desire to protect our children, and everyone around us. A hope and an expectation that things will always make sense, that the parts of the engine don't operate by themselves. That somebody is out to get somebody else, and that we are all bystanders on the fringes of one or several wars that may never be won but that at least can be fought. I think it's idealistic and I think it's naïve, but we believe in these conspiracies because the alternative is a chaotic, determinist universe that is so arbitrary it hurts.

But consider fast food, leading our nation to the top of the charts in heart disease and diabetes: I think we can all agree the demonic descendants of Ray Kroc are not engaged in a conspiracy of any kind, beyond financial success. They locate and exploit their demographic, and things and people fall through the cracks. Junk food's negative health effects lie at the intersection of human choice and the massive dynamic of marketing, and we only see in hindsight what we've done to ourselves.

It is my suggestion that *Fringe* illustrates a war identical to those real-world concerns—one between creative and destructive science, between the better and lesser angels of our search for knowledge. It uses the framework of a sci-fi procedural to explore these questions and fabricated conspiracies from every possible angle, so that what seems to be a conspiracy is revealed, over the course of years, as simply the chaotic by-product of personal choices.

What begins in the first season as a fight against the dark future threatened by the ZFT, one that reveals surprising secrets about Bell and Bishop's untempered explorations, shifts to a story about an alien universe bent on our destruction through science, and then shifts again to a story about two teams of heroes attempting to undo the havoc wreaked by one side's exuberance and the other side's paranoia. It is an escalating war, using science both factual and fabulous, that can only be resolved through the one thing neither side thinks it can safely allow: honest communication between the universes.

Again and again, we see rocks turned over in the show's quest to deconstruct and resolve this basic moral structure: good guys become bad guys, past miracles become acts of vicious hubris, creation becomes destruction. But also, and more to the point, beauty arises from horror, destruction begets creation, our enemy becomes our victim. Interaction between the parallel worlds, as well as flashbacks in both universes, show both the kind and hopeful reasoning behind the horrors we've seen and all the petty and ugly personal reasons for the greatest scientific triumphs.

Science Fiction as Self-Hating Prophecy

As science-fiction fans, we're biased toward pro-science and pro-experimentalism in our mental constructs. The genre is built on Verne, Gernsback, and Wells, entirely and endlessly excited by possibility. The first science-fiction television shows, like the Star Trek series—in particular the first two series—are also based entirely upon the joy of endless exploration: to learn more, to climb higher, to go boldly, to understand and befriend every corner of the Universe. In them, the Universe is knowable, and there is nothing that cannot eventually be understood.

But within science fiction, reaching back as far as the Industrial Revolution and into crannies as far-flung as Lovecraftian cosmic horror and Huxley/Orwell dystopian nightmares, there is also the opposite impulse. A massive dynamic of hubris that starts with Dr. Frankenstein and ends with Dr. Walter Bishop: Mad Scientist. The anti-Verne.

What has always set Walter apart, and thus set apart the show, is his constant search for redemption. His science, in the present day, is based in the idea of closing the loops and gaps (literally, now) that he opened during his heyday of pure (and horrific) science. The Pattern and its adherents tell us this specifically: *Zerstörung durch Fortschritte der Technologie*, the dark grimoire of bastard science from which the ZFT organization takes its name, literally translates as *Destruction through Technological Progress*.

For a science-fiction show, made for mainstream and science-fiction fans, I can't think of a more bizarre principle. In order to succeed as entertainment, the show must also be enjoyable to watch. It cannot be too fatalistic. Destruction through techno-logical progress? Well, then, why don't we all just pack up and go home?

Because it's the imagination that has led us into these traps, and it's the imagination that will lead us out again. This is not a story about destruction through technological progress, but a story about redemption for past hubris *through* techno-logical progress. It is a story about doing what past genera-tions have always done, picking at the threads of past mistakes and turning over those rocks and seeing what miracles we can make in the wreckage of what has gone before, without scribbling over the past.

A science-fictional story acknowledging that we are only ever moving forward.

My Mother the War

Massive Dynamic was Bishop and Bell's greatest achievement of mad scientism, pure science set free through a pure profit motive.[1] Its presence thus completes a sort of philosophical love triangle with the FBI and Walter. Government on one side, pure capitalism on the other, science forever stuck in the middle—but benefitting from, rather than being impeded by, both.

By placing Walter at the intersection of government and corporate interests—and now, in the latest season, into stronger leadership roles in both than he's held since the '80s—the

---

1 While officially Bell built Massive Dynamic while Walter was in the hospital, the company and philosophy were predicated on their work together.

present-day series gives us, in strong relief, the stakes all science and progress are really playing: that while exuberant science plays well with both corporate interests and governmental control, it's the role of the scientist him- or herself to provide the ethical sense that neither government nor industry are built to protect.

Classically, in sci-fi, the government is often a negative force, using the scientific discoveries that it can and quashing those it feels are too threatening. More recently, beginning with the cyberpunk movement, you see the same sort of suspicion about corporations, which have no purpose other than to protect their interests and so become mercenary in their dealings. (Whether or not there's even a useful division between the government and corporate sectors is a revolutionary conversation we can't have right now, but you have a point.)

Utopian fantasies like Star Trek—or JFK's Space Race, for a real-world example—attempt to reverse the narrative of opposition to governmental interference by showing how science and governance can work together toward a brighter future, highlighting the best aspects of both. Likewise, real-world examples of various pure-science initiatives like Google's X-Prize and other high-stakes "outside the box" scientific competitions attempt to undo sixty years of our wariness toward corporations in a way that is both transparent and marketing-savvy.

This is the role that Massive Dynamic attempts to fulfill: to make its money and retain its influence while building a brighter, if perhaps scarier, future, one in which the superhuman and the fantastical close ranks to protect us all, with or without our permission, like so much vortex amber. Without the advances Massive Dynamic made possible, there would be no ZFT, and

Over There would be safe, it's true. There would be no war. Peter would never have been stolen; Olivia and the cortexiphan children would have stayed simple prodigies. No shape-shifters with those horrible tongue-depressor things, no scary ghost-typewriter messages, no reason for Them to come to Us at all. No holes in their universe, no innocents locked in their nightmarish amber prisons.

But without Massive Dynamic and the work on Walter and Bell's part that preceded it, there's also no Olivia as we know her, because there are no cortexiphan children needed to defend Us. There's no Peter as we know him, because he is dead. These two children of the lesser gods of Massive Dynamic, twisted and made beautiful in equal amounts by the mad science of their "parents": Peter as the fulfillment of the First People prophecies, capable of saving one world even though it will mean destroying the other, and Olivia as the most central success of the entire cortexiphan program, our best hope for cross-universe understanding. Their existence in some ways defines the necessity of Walter's quest to atone for his past thought crimes, and it's my belief that he will eventually be redeemed through his children, as parents always are.

One of the first things that interested me about the show was the slowly revealed, complex, and beautiful relationship between Massive Dynamic's big three—Walter, William, and Nina—and its presumably intentional resemblance to the classic Watson/Crick/Franklin love triangle, without which we'd have no DNA and thus no gene therapy, no genetic screening . . .

Genetic manipulation is an easy one to think about, in terms of creation/destruction (or the third, most terrifying determinist possibility, in which nothing we do actually matters: in which our course is "fated," whether by genes or prophecy). And so personally, the historical triangle between these three characters made me understand the show's themes much better than I previously had, back when I thought the show was just about hot people solving various gross X Files. Bell, Bishop, and Sharp are a modern-day Watson/Crick/Franklin, whose past dabbling has created technologies that now threaten us all.

While Walter's need for redemption has caused him irreparable damage—from his self-prescribed lobotomy to his ongoing dissociative drug addictions—we've also seen just how much William Bell was willing to sacrifice for his own atonement. While we've known Walter as a lovable bumbler and, for the most part, only heard about his Mad Science evils, Olivia's meeting with Bell provided an opposite effect: we only knew of Bell as the Bad Guy, until we met him in his loneliness Over There. Nina, once an icicle colder and harder than Olivia herself, has shown a marked predilection for compassion and affection as we've grown to know Massive Dynamic, and thus Nina, better and better—and so we see what the need for redemption has cost her, as well. All three have been transformed in our eyes.

These examples, also rare in a sci-fi show, of investigating characters until we have eliminated them as Bad Guys, eliminated "Them" altogether, are key for a show about resolving the theoretically unresolvable: how to save both universes. Just as we weren't sure about Nina's, or Bell's, motives until we looked closer, we were told again and again that Here and There cannot coexist. Those broken snow globes we keep seeing everywhere, the ZFT and First People manuscripts, all suggest that there must be a winner and a loser in the war between Here and Over There.

But the loops Walter's little family of scientists spend each week closing suggest something very different: that if there is a loser, it is going to be Us. Even if we win—even if we triumph over Them—we lose, because we are Them, and they are Us. And therefore, there must not be a loser. Our efforts must be bent on finding a solution that moves us forward without sacrificing anything.

The Hive Queen and the Hegemon

There is a trend in serial television, going back further than *Buffy* but only really noticeable around the time her influence started showing up in more mainstream fare, in which the narrative function of the antagonist has changed remarkably. Once, going back to the beginning of all stories, the villain provided conflict, the hero resolved the conflict, and the story ended. White Hats, Black Hats, Justice: Thesis, Antithesis, Big Fight.

What *Buffy*, *Dollhouse*, *The O.C.*, *Gossip Girl*, *Lost*, *Alias*, *Farscape*, and *Babylon 5* have to tell us, just to name a few (and you might notice a trend or two in there!), is that we're past that now. Our brains, our understanding of global interrelation, our cultural outgrowing of simple bigotry, the paradigm shift away from simple nationalist WWII thinking into post–Cold War complexity, all of these add up to the new idea expressed by each of those shows in their own way: the enemy is the enemy *only as long as you don't know him.*

You may never become friends, you may disagree on many a topic, but short of mutually assured destruction the only way out is through, as Robert Frost said. And the only way through is no longer to consider genocide—the natural endpoint of war as we commonly understand it—an appropriate goal.

And by love, for the purposes of this paragraph at least, what I mean is knowledge. Orson Scott Card (who could learn a little bit from his earlier writings, this late in the day) illustrated these ideas at play brilliantly in his books *Ender's Game* and *Speaker for the Dead*, both of which suggest that we can only destroy what we know utterly, and only know utterly what we come to love.

Absolute knowledge of Them gives one the power of destruction but also the power of creation, because absolute knowledge of Them makes them into another kind of Us. And that, taken to its limit—knowing someone *absolutely*—is as powerful a description of love as any.

Course Correction

And that—love—is what makes the Over Here/Over There storyline so intense. The affection and familial bonds of Walter's little cow-family of scientists and soldiers have always been at the forefront of the show, but for at least the first season this seemed only like a sort of seasoning, that J.J. Abrams touch that would set it apart from other shows—and take into account the ways we interact with our television now. (Without Mulder and Scully, their chemistry and yearning, would there have been a show at all?)

Being given a chance to know, and to love, the denizens of Over There—in fact, the blameless world of wonders and kindness and harsh decisions that it's proven to be—our perspective surrounding the entire show assumes another shape. Just as when we learned the author of the ZFT manuscript, or why Peter glows, or what became of the cortexiphan children, we're invited to completely and irrevocably reinvestigate the entire preceding story and see it in a new light.

While the actions of Fringe Over There seem extreme and, in many cases, cruel, we've now learned by living their day-to-day lives with them that their existence is precious. They've got zeppelins! A laughing Olivia, wonderful Lincoln, and living Charlie: taxi-drivers with unearthly amounts of compassion and kindness. They've got a Walter less driven mad than driven terrifyingly sane by his losses and responsibilities.

And as we grow to learn and understand Over There, our experience as viewers is recapitulated in the characters' own understandings. If the First People writings are true, if those snow globes really are on a collision course, we must step outside our own biases and see the truth: that of the two universes, we are the bad guys. We are the aggressors, we are the selfish kidnappers, we are the ones burning ants with a magnifying glass, we have caused the vortices Over There and the Pattern Here. If one universe represents Creation and the other Destruction, things have gone very dark indeed at this late hour, because we both know which we've made ourselves.

The show's always been about taking our lumps for that, of course. But now that we have all the details, the story retroactively blossoms into something new: not a tale about what we did, or the ways our unchecked science is destroying Them (or, in the real world, our own humanity and environment), but about *what happens next*. Because there is no going back, but only ever moving forward.

Like Time's Arrow in physics, technological progress only ever moves forward. Accepting that responsibility, as the players at both Fringe and Massive Dynamic are discovering, removes the context of blame and shame from the narrative altogether. There is no collision course, but only ever course *correction*. We can't unbreak the sky—or Olivia, or Peter, or Walter—but we can heal them. It's our duty: that's what growing up is, that's what compassion means. The future, as sci-fi writer Warren Ellis has said more than once, is *always better than the past*.

Creation Through Technological Progress

The Mad Scientist lives at the fringe between the innate creativity of pure science and the potential for destruction that always comes with it, where we find the chance to use those tools to heal us all. Destruction to burn off what doesn't work, and Creation to build something new from the parts that do. That's the very definition of progress, which ends worlds every time.

A quest for redemption can only get you so far, as Walter is learning. The one thing shame will not do for you is give you room to move forward. At some point we must forgive our scientific excesses in order to find the science to solve the problem, which we cannot do if we're constantly afraid the next lamp we rub will release annihilation. Because dystopias and anti-science stories, like the one *Fringe* seemed once to be, are only stops on the way to a greater truth. Given sufficient time, any story resolves itself: any villain, Us or Them, is only ever something to face on the way to a greater compassion.

Which would be pat, and glib—looking at it on the page now, it seems crudely reductive—which is why the show has to give us that story from every angle. Anchor us in the sudden idea that we're the bad guys in order to give us a greater understanding of Them Over There, so that we root not for Justice but for Synthesis. Give us a second Olivia we—and Peter—can love just as much. Give us a Walter in full command of his powers and show us the hard choices he's forced to make.

Given two choices it's our natural inclination to pick one—and it's a particularly American viewpoint that says "no choice is still a choice"—but what we sometimes forget is that it's possible to choose *both*. In the fullness of context, in a story given sufficient time to resolve itself, both is the only possible choice.

And so the show's exploration of scientific ethics—the profit motive of the evil corporation, the coldly measured containment tactics of the arbitrary government, the selfish motivations of the superstar Mad Scientist—once again flips over, revealing the only way out.

It's in the decades of research and absurdly plentiful resources of Massive Dynamic, always willing to provide that last clue or one more jealously guarded secret. It's in the good hearts and strong wills of Fringe Division, on both sides of the trembling glass. It's in the love that Walter and his "children" feel for one another, and in their tested and retested ability to forgive their "parents" for the sins of the past.

I think Winston Churchill would be fond of our team, our little family. "Generous, and true, and also fierce" fairly describes them all, each and every one. From fierce Olivia to brave Peter, to the generosity of Astrid and the limitless compassion of the family they've chosen, the way Walter fights for his family and his sanity, and for the recompense of everything he did when he was young, Churchill would be impressed.

Because there is no harm we can do the world that cannot be healed, in time, using the exact same tools that wounded her. The way out, for both the show's universes and for our own troubled interaction with scientific progress and what it's done to our world, has only ever been through. And that means compassion, and above all *knowledge*: the things our embattled scientists always valued above all else. Love, in another disguise: the massive dynamic.

Or, as Peter eventually puts it in the season-three finale: "This isn't a war that can be won. Our two worlds are inextricable. If one side dies, we all die. So I've torn holes in both the universes, and they lead here. To this room. A bridge, so that we can begin to work together to fix . . ."

And then they're left in the wreckage, once he's been forgotten, and of course it's Olivia who finishes his thought: "Whatever you've both done, we're here now. So maybe it's time we start to fix it."

Or maybe even simpler than that: "Yes, the First People, Walter.

"But the First People are *us*."

> **JACOB CLIFTON** is a writer in Austin, Texas. His critical and analytical work writing about television and film can be found at www.TelevisionWithoutPity.com and www. jacobclifton.com.

ABOUT THE EDITOR

KEVIN R. GRAZIER, PHD, has been a research scientist at NASA's Jet Propulsion Laboratory (JPL) for the past fifteen years, most of which was spent on the Cassini/Huygens Mission to Saturn and Titan. At JPL he has written mission planning and analysis software that won both JPL- and NASA-wide awards. In addition to working in spacecraft operations, his research areas include numerical method development and long-term large-scale computer simulations of Solar System dynamics, evolution, and chaos.

Dr. Grazier is currently the Science Advisor for the SyFy Channel series *Eureka*, the pilot *Battlestar Galactica: Blood and Chrome*, and the NBC series *The Event* and *The Zula Patrol*. He performed the same role for four seasons on the Peabody Award winning *Battlestar Galactica*, and co-authored the book *The Science of Battlestar Galactica*. He was the editor and a contributing author for the anthologies *The Science of Dune* and *The Science of Michael Crichton*.

Dr. Grazier is also very active in bringing the wonders of science and space to the public. He teaches classes in basic astronomy, planetary science, cosmology, the search for extraterrestrial life, and the science of science fiction at UCLA, Santa Monica College, and College of the Canyons. He has appeared on several episodes of History Channel's *The Universe*. Through various outreach programs, he speaks to thousands of K-12 students every year, and yearly serves on multiple NASA educational product review panels.

Dr. Grazier earned BS degrees in computer science and geology, and an MS degree in physics, at Purdue University; a BS in physics at Oakland University; and his doctoral research was at UCLA in geophysics and space physics. Feeling under-educated, he's finishing a certificate in Television Screenwriting from UCLA.

He lives in Sylmar, CA with a mischief of rats, a flock of psitticines, and Kermit the Dog.

ACKNOWLEDGMENTS

The publisher would like to thank the following advance readers for their assistance with the manuscript:

Ashley Doran
Wayne Henderson
Gian-Carlo Parico
Leisa Winrich
Brandon Winrich

Want *More* Smart Pop?

www.smartpopbooks.com

» Read a new free essay online everyday

» Plus sign up for email updates, check out our upcoming titles, and more

 Become a fan on Facebook:
www.smartpopbooks.com/facebook

 Follow us on Twitter:
@smartpopbooks

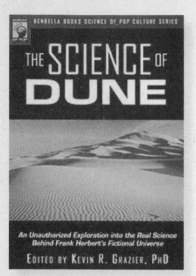

The Science of Dune

An Unauthorized Exploration into the Real Science Behind Frank Herbert's Fictional Universe

EDITED BY KEVIN R. GRAZIER, PHD

In this analysis of the bestselling science fiction adventure of all time, authors explore all aspects of *Dune*, including the fascinating scientific speculations ranging from physics and chemistry to ecology and evolution, from human psychology and mental potential to technology and genetics.

9781933771281 | Trade Paperback | $17.95 US/ $22.95 CAN | December 2007

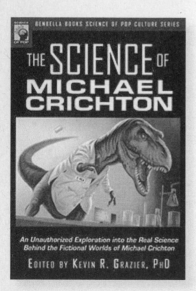

The Science of Michael Crichton

An Unauthorized Exploration into the Real Science behind the Fictional Worlds of Michael Crichton

EDITED BY KEVIN R. GRAZIER, PHD

The Science of Michael Crichton examines the amazing inventions of Crichton's books and lifts up the hood, revealing the science underneath. In intelligent and well-thought essays, scholars and experts decide what Crichton gets right and what he gets wrong. They examine which Crichton imaginings are feasible and which are just plain impossible.

9781933771328 | Trade Paperback | $17.95 US/ $19.95 CAN | February 2008